Simon and Alis

delicious
dishes
without red meat

chicken, fish and vegetarian recipes

NEW
HOLLAND

This edition published in 2002 by
New Holland Publishers (NZ) Ltd

Auckland • Sydney • London • Cape Town

218 Lake Road, Northcote
Auckland, New Zealand

14 Aquatic Drive, Frenchs Forest
NSW 2086, Australia

86–88 Edgware Road, London W2 2EA
United Kingdom

80 McKenzie Street, Cape Town 8001
South Africa

First published in 1995 by C.J. Publishing

Cover Design: Sue Attwood

Design: Rob Di Leva

Editor: Barbara Nielsen

Food Stylist: Alison Holst

Home Economists: Alison Holst, Jane Ritchie
and Dee Harris

Props: Kathy Heath

ISBN: 1-86966-008-0

Printed through Bookbuilders, Hong Kong

1 3 5 7 9 10 8 6 4 2

Cover photo: Roasted Chicken Legs and
Summer Vegetables (page 57)

Preface

Over recent years there have been dramatic shifts in eating patterns – no longer do most of the population regularly sit down to meals of meat and three vegetables. Instead, different eating patterns are emerging.

One of the fastest-growing groups is that of people who are eating little or no red meat, whose meals are based on chicken, fish and vegetarian dishes. This has come about for a number of reasons. For some people it may be just a matter of personal ethics. Others are reducing their red meat consumption because of medical advice. Some people, especially the young and elderly, simply enjoy the milder flavours and softer textures of what is often described as semi-vegetarian food. The cost of chicken compared to red meat is a consideration for many people – as is a widely held perception that chicken is easier to cook than red meat. What's more, many home cooks feel that chicken and fish are very quickly cooked.

Whatever the reasons for this increase in the numbers of people eating less red meat, it is now a well-established eating habit, which has been borne out by the ongoing success of *Meals Without Meat* (first published in 1990). Sales of this book are now in excess of 250,000, and we continue to receive letters and comments from people who enjoy the recipes in it.

But for those who continue to enjoy chicken and fish in their everyday diets, *Delicious Dishes Without Red Meat* (first published several years ago as *Meals Without Red Meat*) offers a wide variety of recipes, especially suitable for households where one or more members prefer meals without red meat.

Important Information

For best results use a standard metric (250ml) cup and standard metric spoons when using the recipes in this book.

1 metric teaspoon holds 5ml   1 metric tablespoon holds 15ml

All the cup and spoon measures are level, unless otherwise stated. (Rounded or heaped measures will upset the balance of ingredients.)

When measuring flour, spoon it into the measure lightly, and level it off without shaking or banging the cup, since this packs down the flour and means that too much is used. Small quarter and half-cup measures are useful for measuring these quantities of flour.

Most butter quantities are given by weight. Small amounts of butter are measured by tablespoon.

1 tablespoon of butter weighs 15 grams

Other important measures and cooking times

cm	centimetre	g	gram	C	Celsius
ml	millilitre	kg	kilogram	l	litre

Microwave cooking times vary, and cannot be given precisely. Microwave instructions have been given for a 650 watt microwave oven with a turntable.

High	**100% power**	**Medium**	**50% power**
Medium High	**70% power**	**Defrost**	**30% power**

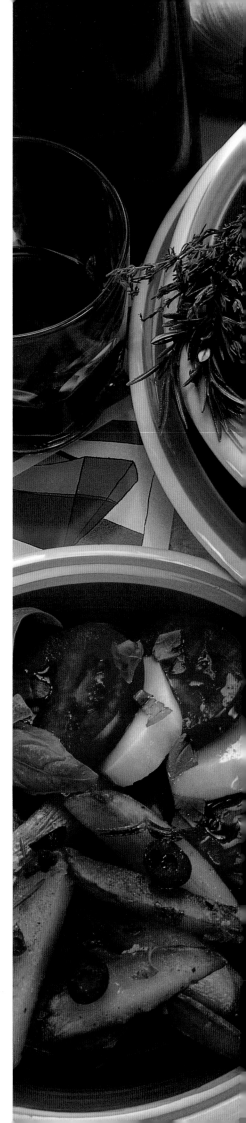

Contents

Soups

You can make wonderful (and often inexpensive) soups based on fish, chicken or vegetables, pulses (dried peas or beans) and grains.

Soups taste even better after standing, so you can make them ahead and refrigerate or freeze them ready for later reheating.

Serve your soups in small amounts for meal starters, or in generous quantities for the main part of the meal.

Garnishes and accompaniments make your soups extra special. For starters, concentrate on colourful garnishes and contrasting textures — a few small crunchy croutons or small crackers, herb sprigs, a swirl of cream or yoghurt, or a sprinkling of paprika or cayenne.

When soup is the main part of your meal, give it star treatment by serving it with crusty rolls or one large country-style loaf (both reheated in your oven), freshly made toast, bubbly toasted cheese savouries or sandwiches, or interesting savoury muffins. You might also like to pass around a tray of optional soup additions — chopped tomatoes, peppers, and/or avocado, toasted pinenuts, sunflower or pumpkin seeds, grated parmesan, snipped coriander leaves, tiny croutons, sour cream or yoghurt, and extra chilli for those who like it very hot!

For stock-based soups, you have the choice of homemade stock, stock bought ready to use, or that which is mixed from instant powders and cubes.

Always taste soup before you serve it, adjusting the seasonings carefully. Nobody wants soup which is too salty, but underseasoned soup can taste flat and boring.

◀ *Lentil Soup with Coriander Leaves (page 11)*

CREAM OF MUSSEL SOUP

This creamy gourmet soup has a lovely flavour, similar to that of oyster soup, and is cheap enough to serve often.

For 4 servings:
500–600g live mussels
mussel stock made up to 3 cups with milk
1 clove garlic, finely chopped
2 Tbsp butter
3 Tbsp flour
¼ tsp freshly grated nutmeg
salt and pepper

Check mussels, discarding any that are cracked or that do not shut if tapped. Steam them in about ¼ cup of water in a covered pot or pan until they open. (If overcooked, they shrink and toughen.)

Strain the liquid from the pan, and make it up to 3 cups with milk.

In a clean pot, cook the garlic in butter until straw-coloured. Stir in flour and nutmeg and cook until bubbling, then add half the milk mixture. Stir until thick and boiling, add remaining liquid then repeat. Simmer for 2–3 minutes, then remove from heat.

Purée the mussels in a food processor, adding some of the sauce from the pot to thin the purée. Press this through a sieve into the sauce, and discard solids. Mix well and season to taste. Just before serving, gently reheat without boiling. (Flavour is best after soup has stood for a few hours.)

Serve as the main part of the meal with Bread Rolls or Sticks (page 104) and a salad (pages 84–87).

SHRIMP AND POTATO CHOWDER

If you keep a can of shrimps in your store cupboard, you can make this popular main-course chunky soup at short notice.

For 4–6 servings:
2 medium-sized onions
1 cup sliced celery (optional)
25g butter
1 cup hot water
1 tsp instant green herbs stock
1 tsp instant chicken stock
3 medium-sized potatoes
200g can shrimps or prawns
2 cups milk
about 2 Tbsp cornflour
parsley and paprika to garnish
salt and pepper

Chop the onions and celery into 1cm squares. Cook gently in the butter in a large covered pot until tender but not browned. Add the water, instant stocks and the potatoes, which have been scrubbed and cut into 1cm cubes. Cover and simmer for 15 minutes or until potatoes are tender.

Add shrimps, liquid from can (unless dark in colour and very strongly flavoured), and milk, and bring to the boil.

Mix cornflour and a little water to a paste and stir in to thicken. Taste and add salt and pepper if necessary. The chowder may be eaten immediately, but its flavour improves on standing for an hour or more. Reheat carefully when required. (If no can liquid is added, extra seasoning will be needed.)

Variation:
Replace shrimps with a can of salmon.

Garnish with paprika and chopped parsley and serve with French Bread or Focaccia (page 104).

CREAMY FISH CHOWDER

This main-meal chowder is well worth the several steps involved, and is a good way to serve less-expensive whole fish.

For 4–6 servings:
3 Tbsp butter
1 large onion, chopped
2 stalks celery, sliced
1 or 2 carrots, sliced
1 cup water
2 tsp instant green herbs or chicken stock
about ½ cup corn
about ½ cup frozen peas
400–600g fish
½ cup white wine or water
3 Tbsp flour
1–2 cups milk
fresh herbs to garnish

Melt 1 tablespoon of the butter in a pot, stir in the onion, celery and carrots, cover and cook gently for 1–2 minutes.

Add the water and instant stock, and cook until the vegetables are tender, then add the corn and peas and cook for a little longer.

In another, larger pot, cook the fish in the water or wine until it flakes, then strain the liquid into the vegetables. Flake the fish, discarding skin and bones, and add the flaked fish to the cooked vegetables.

Clean the pot then melt the remaining 2 tablespoons of butter in it, stir in the flour, heating until it bubbles. Add 1 cup of milk and bring to the boil, stirring constantly. Strain in all the liquid from the fish and vegetables and cook until sauce is smooth and boiling, stirring constantly. Add extra milk or water if too thick. Simmer for about 5 minutes then gently stir in the fish and vegetables and check the seasoning. Reheat carefully when ready to serve.

Garnish with fresh herbs and serve with Garlic Bread (page 112).

Cream of Mussel Soup ▶

▲ *Mediterranean Bean Soup*

MEDITERRANEAN BEAN SOUP

*This is a hearty and nourishing soup with a lovely Mediterranean flavour.
It makes a good, substantial meal in cold weather.*

For 6–8 cup servings:
1½ cups haricot or lima beans
2 or 3 cloves garlic, chopped
2 or 3 bay leaves
2 large onions, chopped
2 carrots, chopped
3 stalks celery, chopped
400g can whole tomatoes in juice
1½ tsp salt
¼ cup olive oil
pepper
¼ cup chopped parsley
1 tsp brown sugar (optional)

Soak the beans in 10 cups of cold water overnight. Add the garlic and bay leaves and simmer for 30 minutes. Add onions, carrots and celery and simmer for a further 30 minutes, until the beans are very soft and the vegetables tender.

Chop the tomatoes and add them with their juice to the cooked beans. Add salt, olive oil, plenty of pepper and the chopped parsley.

Allow to stand for a few hours for best flavour, then reheat and adjust seasonings, adding about a teaspoon of

brown sugar if you think it needs it. Remove the bay leaves and serve. Freeze leftovers if you like.

Variation:
Purée all or half of the solids in the soup to vary the texture.

Serve with crusty, solid bread. Our favourites are Focaccia or Bread Sticks (page 104).

...ORIANDER LEAVES

...ges 6–7.)
...gredients, but tastes very good. Salsa
...s it especially interesting.

...gredients in a
...ld water for
...il lentils are
...ve been
...ill be tender in

...eat oil in a large
...celery and
...pieces about the

size of the lentils, and cook, without browning, for about 10 minutes.

While both the above are cooking, chop the garlic and add half to each mixture. Add the oreganum and cumin to the frypan and cook for a few minutes longer.

Tip the mixture from the frypan into the lentils and simmer for 15 minutes longer. Remove from the heat. Take out the bay leaves and chillies, add the coriander leaves and vinegar, then add salt and black pepper to taste. Freeze what is not to be used immediately.

Serve with Tomato Salsa (page 114).

...BARLEY BROTH

...asty, filling and comforting soup — just
...used to make!

...he onion and garlic
...r about 5 minutes.

...g homemade or
...k diluted with
water, or 2–3 teaspoons instant chicken stock in water. Add the next five ingredients. Add the raw chicken if you want chunks of chicken in the soup, or add a chicken back (frame) for extra body and flavour, if you like.

Bring to boil then simmer gently for 45 minutes. Remove chicken, cube flesh

and return it to soup, then add parsley.

Soup will thicken and flavour will develop if soup is left to stand after cooking, but it is good straight away, too. Add extra water if necessary, and adjust seasonings just before serving.

Freeze for later use if desired.

Serve for main part of meal, or as starter course. Good with toast, Rolls (page 104), Crostini (page 112) or toasted cheese sandwiches.

...cup...
5 cups chicken stock or water
1 cup chopped carrots
1 cup chopped celery
1 potato, chopped
½ tsp thyme
½ tsp oreganum
1 chicken portion (optional)
1 chicken frame (optional)
¼ cup chopped parsley

PUMPKIN-PLUS SOUP

This 30-minute pumpkin soup is interesting and different. The kumara makes it smooth and creamy, and the peanut butter adds interest to the flavour.

For 6–8 servings:
2 Tbsp butter
1 large onion, finely chopped
2 cloves garlic, chopped
½ tsp curry powder
½ tsp crushed coriander seed*
⅛–¼ tsp chilli powder
½ tsp salt
250g (1 large) roughly cubed kumara
250g roughly cubed pumpkin
4 cups water
2 tsp instant chicken stock
1 rounded household Tbsp peanut butter
Grind whole coriander seeds for stronger flavour.

Melt the butter in a pot, add the chopped onion and garlic and cook gently in the butter without browning.

Stir in the curry powder, coriander seeds, as much chilli powder as you want for hotness, and salt, and cook for 1 minute longer. Add vegetables, weighed after preparation (do not use more kumara than pumpkin, because the soup will be too sweet).

Add the water and instant stock, and simmer gently for 15–20 minutes or until the vegetables are tender, then stir in the peanut butter.

Purée the soup in a food processor, blender or mouli, or mash it with a potato masher to get the consistency you want.

Note:
The larger amount of chilli powder (ground chilli) gives a hotness stronger than most children could cope with. Use half the quantity for a family soup.

Serve with small, crisp Croutons (page 112) or garnish with a spoonful of unsweetened plain yoghurt, swirled on top.

EASY VEGETABLE SOUP

You can make really easy soups very quickly when you start with smooth-textured root vegetables.

For 2–3 servings:
1 onion, very finely chopped
1 clove garlic
pinch of curry powder
2 tsp butter or oil
400–500g kumara or pumpkin or
    parsnips or Jerusalem artichokes
¼–½ cup water
about ¼ tsp salt or ½ tsp instant stock
1–2 cups milk

To cook in a microwave oven:
Put the onion, garlic, curry powder and butter or oil in a roasting bag and cook on High (100% power) for 2 minutes. Peel one or more of the vegetables to be used, cut them into 2cm chunks, add them and the smaller amount of water to the bag. Close bag loosely with a rubber band, leaving a finger-sized hole, then microwave for 4–6 minutes or until the vegetables feel soft when pinched through the bag.

To cook in a pot:
Cook the onion, garlic, curry powder and butter in a medium-sized pot on medium heat for 1–2 minutes, add the cubed vegetables with the larger amount of water, and simmer in the covered pot until the vegetables are tender when pierced with a knife.

Purée the mixture in a food processor or blender with the salt or instant stock until smooth, thinning to creamy soup consistency with milk. Pour through a sieve to remove any lumps, then heat to desired temperature and serve.

Variations:
• Add a little cream or cream cheese with the milk.
• Purée in a mouli or mash with a potato masher or fork.
• Add a spoonful of smooth peanut butter with the milk.
• Use coconut cream and water to replace the milk.
• Cook herbs or spices with the vegetables.

Serve in mugs or bowls with toast, Bread Rolls (page 104) or Garlic Bread (page 112).

SMOOTH AND CRUNCHY CREAM SOUP

This smooth soup is good hot or cold. Add crisp green vegetables to the hot or chilled soup just before it is served.

For 4 servings:
250g (2 fairly large) potatoes
2 cups milk
1 clove garlic, finely chopped
¼ tsp salt
½ cup cream cheese
¼ cup dry white wine
¼ cup cream
¼ cup each of chopped watercress,
    lettuce, spinach, grated cucumber
2 spring onions, finely chopped
¼ cup chopped snow pea sprouts

Peel and cube the potatoes and cook gently in the milk with the garlic and salt until tender.

Measure the cream cheese, wine and cream into a food processor, add the hot cooked potato, and process until smooth. Add the cooking liquid etc. after potato is puréed. (Sieve to get the smoothness you require.) Taste and adjust seasonings.

Chill the vegetables you intend to add to the soup. Chop or grate them just before they are to be added to the soup, moments before serving.

Serve hot or refrigerate the creamy soup until well chilled. Sprinkle with Croutons (page 112) before serving.

FRESH TOMATO SOUP

Made from ripe red tomatoes, this is good either hot or chilled. Add the orange if you feel like something different.

For 4 servings:
600g tomatoes, Italian if possible
1 small onion, finely chopped
2 tsp olive oil
¼ cup white wine
2 cups chicken stock
1 orange (optional)
2 tsp wine vinegar
1 thick slice white bread
6–10 drops Tabasco sauce
¼–½ tsp salt
about 1 tsp sugar
freshly ground black pepper

Pour boiling water over the tomatoes in a bowl. Leave for a minute, until the skin peels easily, then drain, cool in cold water, peel and chop, discarding seeds and watery juice if necessary.

Cook the onion in the oil until soft but not browned. Add the tomatoes, wine and (bought, homemade or mixed-from-instant) stock and simmer for about 5 minutes.

For an orange flavour, finely grate the rind from half an orange. For a garnish, cut small, thin strips of rind from the remaining half orange, and put aside. Put

the grated rind in a shallow bowl with the juice squeezed from the orange, bread, and wine vinegar. When bread is soft, mash to a pulp with a fork, then stir or whisk this mixture into the hot soup. Add remaining seasonings, checking to balance the flavours. (If you are not adding orange, mash the bread with a little of the soup.)

If soup is to be served cold, chill it for several hours. Otherwise, reheat it.

Serve topped with the reserved orange zest, or with crisp Croutons (page 112) or with Bread Rolls (page 104).

DOT'S MYSTERIOUS BEER SOUP

*This soup makes a good conversation piece, it has an interesting flavour that is
not easily identified.*

For 6 servings:
2 Tbsp butter
2 large onions, finely chopped
2 large carrots, finely chopped
¼ cup flour
*2 cups chicken stock (or 2 tsp instant
chicken stock plus 2 cups water)*
250g carton cream cheese
about 2 cups lager beer
chopped parsley or chives

Melt the butter in a large pot. Add the
onion to the melted butter and cook for
about 5 minutes over a low heat,
without browning, until quite soft. Add
the carrot and cook for a further 5–10
minutes, until the carrot has softened.

Stir the flour into the cooked onion and
carrot, then add the chicken stock (or
instant stock dissolved in the water). Stir
over a gentle heat until thickened.
Simmer for 5–10 minutes, then cool
slightly before puréeing in a blender or
food processor. Pour back into the pot.

Food-process the cream cheese with
enough beer to mix it to a thin cream,
then combine in the pot with the
vegetable purée and the remaining beer.
Bring to the boil, and adjust seasonings
if necessary.

Garnish with finely chopped parsley or
chives.

*Serve with Bread Sticks (page 104)
Croutons (page 112) or Bread Rolls
(page 104) if desired.*

13

Starters and Light Meals

If you have ever looked through a restaurant menu and thought that the "Starters" looked much more interesting than the "Mains" you should glance through this chapter and see what tantalises your taste buds!

Try one recipe alone, for lunch; make several, so friends you have asked for a glass of wine at lunchtime in the weekend have a choice; serve one for a dinner party starter: or make a careful selection and serve a number of these with a variety of breads and salads for the main part of a casual evening meal.

When you decide to serve several of these for a main meal, make your selection after considering colours, flavours and textures, as well as remembering dietary guidelines. Crisp raw vegetables and crusty breads go well with dips and pates. Many of these recipes may be made ahead — always a help when you have guests coming and 101 things to do!

(There are two chicken liver recipes in this chapter — these are included because they taste good, are relatively inexpensive, and are good sources of iron, a mineral sometimes lacking in semi-veg diets.)

◀ *'Pretend' Pâté (page 17)*

▲ *Chicken Liver Pâté*

CHICKEN LIVER PATE

This pâté is a smooth, rich mixture that uses no bacon or chopped hard-boiled eggs.

400g chicken livers (fresh or frozen)
1/4 cup dry or medium sherry
1 Tbsp brandy or whisky
100g butter
1 large clove garlic
1–2 Tbsp finely chopped onion
1/4 tsp salt
1 Tbsp chopped parsley
1 tsp fresh thyme leaves or 1/2 tsp dried thyme
1 tsp fresh marjoram leaves or 1/2 tsp dried marjoram

Thaw the livers if necessary and cut each into several pieces, discarding any stringy bits. Add the sherry and brandy or whisky and allow to stand for at least 5 minutes.

Melt half the butter in a large frypan, and stir in garlic and onion. Add drained chicken livers, brown lightly on all sides, then stir in the marinating liquid, salt and herbs. Cook until livers are no longer pink in the middle.

In a food processor or blender, process until smooth. Add remaining butter and process again until mixed. Push through a fine sieve if you want a smooth pâté, then pour into one or more dishes and leave to set. Top with a layer of melted butter if desired. (Butter topping helps keep pâté from discolouring.)

Serve with Crostini or Melba Toast (page 112), or crackers.

16

SMOKED FISH PATE

*Quick and easy to make, this pâté turns run-of-the-mill smoked fish into
something special for a summer lunch or dinner starter.*

200g hot-smoked* mackerel or other fish
1 cup cream cheese
1 Tbsp capers
1 tsp caper liquid
clarified butter (optional)
few drops Tabasco or Worcestershire
    sauce

*Hot-smoked fish is cooked during
smoking, so may be eaten 'as is'.*

Remove skin and bones from the fish
fillets if necessary. Break into even-sized
pieces. Process in food processor with
room-temperature cream cheese. Blend
until thick and smooth.

Add capers and liquid, and Tabasco or
Worcestershire sauce. Process only until
capers are finely chopped.

Spoon into one large or individual small
pots. Seal with melted clarified butter if
desired.

Serve within three days.

*Serve with Melba Toast (page 112), or
sliced french bread as a starter or with a
Bread Roll (page 104), crackers or fresh
vegetables for lunch.*

'PRETEND' PATE

*(See photograph pages 14–15.)
This pâté looks and tastes rather like chicken liver pâté,
even though it contains no chicken, nor liver.*

¼ cup olive oil
2 cloves garlic, chopped
1 large onion, chopped
¼ cup celery, chopped
1 cup (100g) chopped walnuts
pinch of chilli powder
¼ tsp thyme
4 hard-boiled eggs
½ tsp salt
freshly ground black pepper

Heat the oil in a small frypan, add the
garlic, onion and celery and cook over
moderate heat until vegetables are
lightly browned.

Add the walnuts and continue to cook
until the walnuts brown slightly. Stir in
the chilli powder and thyme.

Remove from the heat, then transfer
mixture to a food processor fitted with
its metal chopping blade. Process
briefly, then add the roughly chopped
eggs, salt and pepper and process until

the mixture is fairly smooth or whatever
you consider is the pâté texture you
want.

Note:
Because this pâté looks 'meaty', give it a
vegetarian label at a party.

*Serve cold, with Melba Toast or Crostini
(page 112) or crackers, and a selection
of crisp raw vegetables.*

SMOKED SALMON PATE

*Smoked salmon offcuts are considerably cheaper than perfect slices, but have the
same delicious flavour. With small packets of offcuts in your freezer you can
produce a luxury pâté in a short time.*

100g fresh or frozen salmon offcuts
50g room-temperature butter
½–1 tsp Tabasco sauce
2 spring onions, roughly chopped
2–3 tsp chopped fresh dill leaves
    (optional)
¼ cup chopped unskinned telegraph
    cucumber (optional)
2–3 tsp capers (optional)

Bring salmon offcuts to room
temperature (after thawing at a low
power level in a microwave oven if
necessary). Chop finely in a food
processor then add the room
temperature (slightly soft) butter and
process until light-coloured and creamy.

Add the Tabasco sauce and spring
onions with one or more of the optional
ingredients and process enough to mix.

Pack into one or more small dishes. Seal
by pouring melted butter over the
surface if you plan to keep the pâté.

*Serve slightly chilled, so mixture is just
soft enough to spread. Serve on sliced
french bread, Crostini (page 112),
cracker biscuits or Melba Toast (page
112).*

SESAME EGGPLANT DIP

This dip (relish or spread) has an amazing flavour even though it has a rather drab appearance. It is well worth trying, and is addictive!

300g eggplant
1 tsp grated fresh ginger
1 large garlic clove, finely chopped
2 spring onions, finely chopped
1 Tbsp finely chopped fresh coriander
    leaves
1 Tbsp light soya sauce
1 Tbsp wine vinegar
½ jalapeno pepper, finely chopped
1½ tsp sesame oil
1 Tbsp olive or other oil (optional)
1–2 tsp toasted sesame seeds

Cut unpeeled eggplants into small cubes and, as they are prepared, drop them into a small amount of boiling water in a covered pot. Stir after each addition. As soon as they are tender, after 5–10 minutes, drain off any remaining water.

While the eggplant cooks, mix together all the remaining ingredients except the toasted sesame seeds. Add to the warm, drained, cooked eggplant, tossing thoroughly to mix.

If you prefer smaller pieces, chop in a food processor. Refrigerate in a covered container for up to four days.

Serve piled in a bowl, topped with the toasted sesame seeds, and with extra chopped coriander leaves if you like. For dipping serve alongside corn chips, or with Crostini or Melba Toast (page 112).

MEXICAN CHEESE AND TOMATO DIP

Try to keep the ingredients on hand, so you can make this easy, delicious hot dip at short notice. Served with plenty of corn chips it is always popular!

For 4–8 servings:
1 medium-sized onion, chopped
1 green pepper, chopped
1 Tbsp oil
1 Tbsp chopped jalapeno peppers
425g can Mexican Tomatoes
1 Tbsp flour
2 cups grated tasty cheese
¼–½ cup low-fat sour cream
coriander leaves or spring onions for
    garnish

Cook the onion and green pepper in the oil, without browning, for 2–3 minutes.

Add the jalapeno peppers (available in a jar from supermarkets) and tomatoes, and bring to the boil.

Toss the flour through the cheese, then stir into the hot tomato mixture until melted and smooth.

Serve hot, in a shallow dipping bowl, topped with sour cream. Garnish with chopped coriander leaves or finely chopped spring onions.

Variations:
Replace Mexican Tomatoes with whole tomatoes and added cumin and oreganum if necessary.

Serve surrounded by corn chips.

LAYERED FESTIVE DIP

This spectacular layered dip can be prepared up to 24 hours before a party, without the avocado discolouring.

For 6 servings:
2 cloves garlic, finely chopped
¼ tsp chilli powder
1 tsp each ground cumin and oreganum
¼ tsp salt
1 Tbsp oil
440g can baked beans
2 Tbsp tomato paste
1 or 2 avocados
3–4 Tbsp lemon juice
½–1 cup low-fat sour cream
hot chilli sauce to taste
coriander leaves, black olives, spring
    onions and hot chilli sauce to
    garnish

Cook garlic and the seasonings in oil for about one minute. Add baked beans and tomato paste, mashing well as mixture heats through. Remove from the heat and leave to cool. Spread evenly in one or more straight-sided glass dishes.

Mash avocado and lemon juice and spread evenly over the bean mixture.

Season sour cream with chilli sauce, then spread over avocado. Cover and refrigerate until required.

Just before serving, decorate top with chopped coriander leaves, sliced, pitted black olives and/or spring onions and a dribble of hot chilli sauce.

Variation:
Stir 1 cup grated tasty cheese into hot bean mixture.

Serve with corn chips or Crostini (page 112), scooping deep to get several layers.

LENTIL DAHL

This is the tastiest dahl we have ever made.

1 cup red lentils
2½ cups water
1 large onion, chopped
2 cloves garlic, chopped
1 tsp each turmeric, ground coriander,
  ground cumin, grated fresh ginger
1 or 2 small dried chillies, crushed
1 Tbsp oil
1–2 tsp Spice Mix
1 tsp each salt and sugar
2 Tbsp lemon juice
1 Tbsp butter (optional)

Wash and drain the lentils, then simmer them in a covered pot, with the next eight ingredients, for 20–30 minutes, until thick and mushy.

While this cooks, in a small pan heat the oil, add the Spice Mix spices and cook until they brown lightly and smell aromatic. Remove from the heat and add the salt, sugar and lemon juice.

When lentils are almost cooked, stir in the spice mixture. Adjust seasonings to taste, adding a tablespoon of butter if you like. The dahl will thicken on cooling and standing. Serve it warm or cold. Refrigerate in a covered container for up to four days.

Spice Mix:
Mix equal volumes of black mustard seeds, cumin seeds, fennel seeds, and fenugreek. Store in an airtight jar. (If necessary, get the spices from a store stocking Indian foods and ingredients.)

Flatbread Rollups:
Spread dahl on naan or mountain bread. Add grated carrot, lettuce leaves, sliced celery (and grated cheese if you like). Roll up tightly, wrap in plastic cling film until needed, then cut into short lengths with a really sharp knife.

Serve as a dip with Crostini (page 112), as a spread on Bread Rolls (page 104) or thin down as a curry side dish.

19

▲ *Stuffed Grape Leaves*

STUFFED GRAPE LEAVES

Although dolmades, or stuffed grape leaves, may seem most exotic, they are easy and inexpensive to make, if you or your friends have the right things growing in your garden.

For 36 dolmades:
about 40 young grape leaves
1 onion, finely chopped
½ cup olive oil
½ cup uncooked rice
½ cup currants
¼–½ cup pinenuts
¼ cup lemon juice
1–2 Tbsp chopped fresh mint
1–2 Tbsp chopped fresh parsley
1–2 Tbsp chopped fresh dill leaves
1 tsp salt
1 cup water

Put the grape leaves into a pot of boiling water, and hold them under the surface until they will fold easily, without breaking. Cool in cold water.

Cook the onion gently in half the olive oil for 2–3 minutes. Add the rice, currants and pinenuts, stir for a minute longer, then remove from the heat, and add half the lemon juice, two or more of the herbs and the salt.

With the shiny side of the leaves down, put a teaspoon of rice mixture on the centre of each leaf. Fold the stem ends then the sides of the leaf over the filling, and roll up loosely into cylinders.

Arrange the stuffed leaves side by side, in one layer in a baking dish. Drizzle with the remaining oil and lemon juice then pour the water round them. Cover with flat grape leaves then with a lid or foil. Bake at 150°C for 1–1½ hours, or until the rice is cooked and the stuffed leaves are tender. Drain, and cover with plastic cling film and leave to cool. Refrigerate for up to four days.

Serve at room temperature.

CRISPY CHICKEN NOODLE SALAD

This salad is an interesting mixture of lettuce, crisp white noodles and smoked chicken in an Oriental dressing.

For 6 starter-course servings:
400–500g boneless smoked chicken
oil
100g dry rice or bean vermicelli noodles
6–9 cups finely shredded lettuce
1/2 cup chopped spring onions
1/2 cup chopped coriander leaves
3 Tbsp sesame seeds, lightly toasted
1/4 cup pickled ginger, thinly sliced

Lemon-Honey Dressing:
1 tsp finely grated lemon rind
1/4 cup lemon juice
2 Tbsp each of light soya sauce, salad oil, and honey
1 Tbsp each of smooth Dijon mustard and sesame oil
1 clove garlic, very finely chopped

Prepare all ingredients and assemble salad just before serving.

Cut chicken into thin small strips, and chill in a plastic bag until required.

Heat 2cm oil in a deep pan or wok, until smoking. Tear the noodles into 4–6 small handfuls. Add a handful of noodles to the hot oil, turn until puffed up and crisp and very lightly browned, about 30 seconds, then drain well on paper towels. Repeat with remaining noodles. Put aside in a sealed plastic bag if made ahead.

Just before the salad is wanted, shred the lettuce finely and spread it on a wide shallow bowl or platter. Top with the smoked chicken, sprinkle with the spring onion, coriander leaves, sesame seeds, and the ginger. Sprinkle the crisp fried noodles on top.

Shake together in a screw-topped jar the ingredients for the Lemon-Honey Dressing. At the table drizzle dressing over the salad, toss gently to mix the ingredients and serve at once.

Note:
Look in the specialty food section of a large supermarket, or in an Asian food supply store, for the noodles and pickled ginger.

Serve as a starter or with a Bread Roll (page 104) for lunch.

TUNA AND PASTA SUMMER SALAD

Pasta salads always seem popular in hot weather.

For 6–8 servings:
250g pasta
425g can Italian Tomatoes
3 Tbsp olive oil
2 Tbsp wine vinegar
2 tsp sugar
1 tsp salt
2 spring onions, finely chopped
1 cup finely sliced celery
200g can tuna

Cook the pasta in a large pot of boiling (unsalted) water until just tender. When cooked, drain and put hot pasta into a large unperforated plastic bag with all of the remaining ingredients except the tuna. Leave to cool, turning bag at intervals.

Flake the tuna, mix gently with the pasta mixture and leave to stand for at least 10 minutes before serving.

Refrigerate until needed, up to three days.

Note:
Use the oil or brine from the tuna for a stronger fish flavour.

Serve at room temperature for best flavour, but some people prefer it straight from the refrigerator, while others warm it in the microwave. Take your pick!

JACKET WEDGES

These trendy snacks are popular with all age groups. Ring in the changes by adding different spices to flavour them, then serve them with one or more bought or homemade dips — the sky's the limit!

For 3–4 servings:
4 large potatoes (1kg)
3–4 Tbsp olive oil
1 Tbsp light soya sauce
1–2 tsp very finely chopped garlic
1 Tbsp grated parmesan cheese
1/2 tsp salt

Scrub but do not peel the potatoes. Cut each potato into about eight wedges lengthways. Put the wedges into a bowl of cold water until all are prepared then drain and pat dry on paper towels.

In a bowl mix together the olive oil, soya sauce, garlic, parmesan and salt. Using your fingers, gently turn the dried potatoes in this mixture to coat them thoroughly. Stand the wedges skin-side down in a large baking dish, preferably one with a non-stick surface.

Bake at 200°C for 35–40 minutes, or until tender and golden brown.

Variations:
Mix other seasonings with the oil, to suit your taste. Try for example: 2 tsp ground cumin, 1 tsp oreganum, 1/4–1/2 tsp chilli powder, 1/4 tsp thyme or 1/2 tsp Tabasco sauce or 1 tsp curry powder, or sprinkle with specially formulated spice mixtures to give particular ethnic flavours.

Serve hot or warm with dips such as guacamole, Tomato Salsa (page 114), Satay Sauce (page 115), Pesto (page 113), Mayonnaise (page 115), Quick Tapenade (page 113).

FRITTATA

A frittata may be described as a solid omelet, in which vegetables (often including potatoes) are cooked.

For 3–4 servings:
½ large red onion, sliced
2–3 Tbsp olive oil
3 Roasted Peppers (yellow and red)
3 eggs
¼ tsp salt
about 1 tsp chopped fresh herbs
about 2 Tbsp parmesan cheese (optional)

Cook onion in oil in a covered, medium-sized pan, until transparent. Add sliced Roasted Peppers (page 23) and heat through, turning occasionally. Beat eggs with salt, herbs and parmesan cheese.

Pour egg mixture over vegetables in the pan. Jiggle pan to distribute egg mixture, and cook over moderate heat, lifting sides regularly to let uncooked mixture run underneath, until all the egg mixture sets. Dry the top of the frittata under the grill if necessary.

Variations:
Replace Roasted Peppers with 2–3 cups of one or more other cooked vegetables, such as potatoes, carrots, corn, green beans, kumara, leeks or broccoli. Proceed as above.

Replace Roasted Peppers with tender raw vegetables, such as mushrooms, zucchini, peas, spinach and broccoli. To speed up their cooking, cover the pan after you mix them through the partly cooked onions. Adjust heat so vegetables cook without browning and without producing liquid.

Serve hot, warm or at room temperature with a Mixed Green Salad (page 86).

TASTY TARTLETS

These tartlets are ideal for party food or light meals. Try these fillings then invent your own, using this pastry, and this savoury custard to surround it.

For 12 tartlets:
1¼ cups flour
1 tsp baking powder
125g cold butter
½ cup milk
1 tsp wine vinegar

Broccoli and Brie Filling:
well-drained chopped cooked broccoli
small cubes of Brie

Smoked Salmon and Avocado Filling:
small cubes of avocado sprinkled with lemon juice
chopped smoked salmon
chopped dill leaves or spring onion

Savoury Custard:
2 eggs
½ cup milk
½ cup cream
½ tsp salt

Toss the flour and baking powder together in a large bowl. Grate the cold butter coarsely into the flour then toss to distribute it evenly. Mix the milk and vinegar, then slowly add enough of this liquid to the flour mixture to make a fairly firm dough, tossing with a fork to mix. Refrigerate for 5 minutes, then roll out thinly and use to line about a dozen small tartlet tins, or wide, shallow patty pans.

Place the chosen filling lightly into uncooked pastry shells, leaving room for the savoury custard that will surround them.

Mix the Savoury Custard ingredients together until blended. Pour over filling in uncooked tartlets, using about 1½ tablespoons for each, or less if shells are smaller.

Bake at 200°–210°C for about 10 minutes, until pastry is golden brown and filling set and puffed.

Serve warm, reheating if necessary.

EGGS BENEDICT

This rich recipe suits very special occasions! While traditionally served for breakfast (or brunch), they are really good at any time of the day or night!

For 2 large servings:
Hollandaise Sauce
4 eggs
2 English muffins
a few slices of smoked salmon

Make once the recipe of Hollandaise Sauce on page 115.

Prepare four poached eggs, using very fresh eggs if possible. (Eggs may be poached before they are needed, cooled in cold water to stop the yolks from hardening, then reheated by standing in boiling water for several minutes.)

Split and toast two English muffins.

Variation:
Replace smoked salmon with cooked, well-drained, lightly buttered spinach, flavoured with a little nutmeg.

To serve, top each toasted muffin with smoked salmon, hot poached eggs and Hollandaise Sauce.

ROASTED RED PEPPERS

Made when peppers are at their best, these taste as good as they look. Even if you are doubtful — try them!

For 4 servings:
4 red (or yellow) peppers
8 basil leaves
2 cloves garlic, thinly sliced
8 anchovy fillets
about 16 capers
6 medium-sized tomatoes, or canned
*   whole tomatoes*
8–16 black olives
about ¼ cup (extra virgin) olive oil
fresh basil leaves for garnish

Halve peppers lengthways, cutting through the stems so they remain intact. Remove pith and seeds. Lay the peppers in one layer in a shallow roasting dish.

Place a basil leaf and several slices of garlic in the bottom of each pepper. Cut the anchovy fillets into pieces and place on the basil, then divide the capers between the peppers.

If using fresh tomatoes, blanch to remove skins and cut in halves or quarters. Cut peeled or canned tomatoes lengthways, and shake out the seeds and liquid. Place tomatoes, cut side down, in the peppers. Top with the olives. Drizzle 1–2 teaspoons of olive

oil over each halved pepper.

Bake uncovered, at 200°C for about 30 minutes, until the peppers are lightly charred at the edges. Spoon any liquid around the peppers into them. Refrigerate if necessary, and warm to desired temperature before serving or serve at room temperature. Garnish with fresh basil leaves.

Note:
Do not use green peppers for this recipe.

Serve alone or with chunks of Bread Roll (page 104) to mop up all the delicious juices.

23

▲ *Spicy Potato Samosas*

SPICY POTATO SAMOSAS

Filo pastry makes a quick, light, flaky wrapper for these popular savouries.

For 4 servings (8 small samosas):
2 cooked medium-sized potatoes
1 medium-sized onion, diced
1 Tbsp oil
1½ tsp curry powder
1 tsp ground cumin
½ tsp garam masala
½ tsp ground coriander
½–¾ cup frozen peas
about ½ tsp salt
about ½ tsp sugar
juice of ½ lemon
2–3 Tbsp chopped mint or fresh
*   coriander leaves*
6 sheets filo pastry
butter or oil for brushing

Cut the cooked potatoes into 1cm cubes.

In a large frypan, cook the onion in the oil until soft, adding the next four seasonings as the onion cooks. Add the (thawed) peas and about 2 tablespoons of water, cover and cook for a few minutes longer. Stir in the cubed potato, the salt, sugar and lemon juice, mixing everything well, without breaking up the potato completely, then taste critically, adding more salt, sugar and lemon juice if the mixture seems too bland. Stir in the chopped mint or coriander leaves.

To make the filo triangles, layer three sheets of filo pastry, brushing between each with butter or oil. Cut into four strips crossways. Put a spoonful of filling at the top of one strip, then fold the filo over it so the top touches the edge, forming a triangle. Keep folding in triangles to enclose the filling. Repeat with the remaining filo and filling, always using three sheets per 'sandwich'. Brush the tops lightly with a little more butter or oil.

Place triangles on a baking tray. Bake at 200°C for 10 minutes then turn the oven temperature down to 180°C and cook for 15–20 minutes longer until evenly golden brown.

Serve warm, as finger food.

CURRIED CHICKEN SAMOSAS

Deliciously spicy chicken wrapped in triangular filo parcels.

For 12 parcels:
250g minced chicken
1 onion, finely chopped
1 tsp grated fresh ginger
½ tsp chilli powder
½ tsp turmeric
425g can Savoury Tomatoes
1 cup frozen peas
1 tsp garam masala
2 Tbsp chopped coriander leaves
1 Tbsp cornflour
12 sheets filo pastry
melted butter or oil

Put minced chicken and onion into a preheated frypan and brown well, adding the ginger, chilli powder and turmeric as the meat cooks. Add the tomatoes and cook uncovered until almost dry, then add next three ingredients. Cook for 2 minutes longer.

Mix cornflour to a paste with a little cold water and stir into chicken mixture to thicken it. Cool then make 12 chicken-stuffed filo triangles using instructions from previous recipe (page 24) for shaping and baking.

Serve warm, reheating if necessary.

SALMON SURPRISE PACKAGES

These Salmon Surprises give a feeling of lightness and frivolity to a special-occasion meal. They also make a little salmon go a long way.

For 4 servings:
4–8 thin slices smoked salmon or 60g
    smoked salmon offcuts
2 tsp horseradish sauce (optional)
2 Tbsp sour cream
4 cooked medium-sized new potatoes
1 Tbsp chopped spring onion
salt and pepper (optional)
4 slices of soft, mould-ripened cheese
8 sheets filo pastry
about 2 tsp soft butter
4 whole chives or other ties

Chop the salmon into small pieces. Mix with the horseradish sauce, sour cream, the cooked potato chopped into pea-sized pieces, and chopped spring onion. Season lightly, if you like. Keep the cheese slices separate.

Layer two sheets of filo pastry, brushing between the two layers with butter, using about ½ teaspoon per sheet. Cut each sheet in half. Place one half on top of the other, so there are eight more-or-less equidistant corners. Put one-quarter of the prepared filling and one slice of cheese in the centre, then gather up the edges so the filling is surrounded. Tie a long chive (or other tie) around the pastry before baking. Repeat with remaining filo and filling.

Bake in lightly buttered or sprayed sponge-roll pans at 190°C for about 10 minutes, or until lightly browned.

Serve alone as a starter.

CHICKEN LIVER CRACKERS

For a special occasion, make edible filo crackers.

For 6 crackers:
9 sheets filo pastry
melted butter or oil for brushing
12 chives

Chicken Liver and Mushroom Filling:
1 onion, chopped
2 cloves garlic, chopped
25g butter
100g mushrooms, chopped
250g chicken livers
2 tsp fresh thyme leaves
1 tsp flour
2 Tbsp sherry
2 Tbsp cream
salt and pepper

Cook the onion and garlic in butter until lightly browned, add the mushrooms and heat through, then raise the heat and add the halved chicken livers and thyme. When livers are firm but still pink in the middle, stir in the flour, sherry and cream. Break up the livers into smaller pieces and season carefully. Form into six even piles.

Layer three sheets of filo, brushing between each with butter or oil. Cut each 'sandwich' in half, and using one-sixth of the filling, fold up as in the diagram. Pinch the pastry together about 3cm from the ends and fasten each with a knotted chive leaf. Repeat with remaining filo and filling.

Bake at 190°C for about 10 minutes or until lightly browned, then put aside and reheat just before serving, at about the same temperature, until heated through.

Variation:
Fill crackers with one of the other filo fillings given.

Serve alone as a starter.

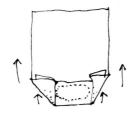

Fish Mains

We often look at the sparkling blue waters which surround us and think how lucky we are to be able to harvest fish from this huge, clean expanse of sea.

Fish is a popular restaurant choice, but as well is a natural convenience food, since it cooks quickly in a variety of ways, is good served plainly, and is delicious when combined with many different seasonings and sauces.

Nearly always, popular fish varieties are the most expensive. It is well worth trying some of the lesser known, less expensive varieties. You can often substitute one for another, especially if you know whether the texture of the cooked flesh is firm, medium or delicate.

Fish with a soft or delicate texture breaks up easily when cooked. A firm, protective coating (such as egg-crumb), on small pieces prevents this.

Medium-textured fish holds its shape when cooked, has fairly large flakes, and may be cooked in all ways.

Firm-textured fish does not separate into flakes when moved about during cooking. It keeps its shape well.

Farmed mussels, excellent value for money, are iron-rich, and delicious served in many ways, as long as they are not overcooked.

Don't overlook cans of fish. These are great value for money, are convenient, ready to eat, and popular with many children.

The following recipes show the versatility of fish. Variety is particularly important when fish is served several times a week.

◀ *Salad Niçoise (page 40)*

BASIC PAN-FRIED FISH

When you have plenty of top-quality, well-flavoured fish (such as fine-textured flatfish fillets), the simplest cooking method is best!

For 1 serving:
about 150g fish
milk (optional)
about ¼ cup flour
about ½ tsp salt
2–3 tsp olive oil
2–3 tsp butter

Trim away any ragged edges of fish. Pat fish dry if necessary. Cut in smaller pieces if too large to cook and turn over easily. When ready to cook, dip fish in a shallow dish of milk (if you like a thicker coating) then turn it in a mixture of flour and salt, on another shallow dish or a paper towel. Pat coating lightly with fingers, if not using milk.

Cook fish in a non-stick pan if possible. Preheat pan over a moderate heat. When fish is ready to cook, swirl a little olive oil over the base of the pan. Add butter and tilt pan as it melts. As soon as

it bubbles, but before it darkens, add fish. Immediately jiggle pan to stop fish sticking to it. Cook over high heat for thin fillets, lower heat for thicker pieces, turning fish once. Fish should be lightly browned and flesh should be milky rather than translucent in the thickest part, when ready. Thin fillets may take as short a time as 45 seconds a side, thicker fillets, slices or cutlets 2–3 minutes per side.

Serve immediately with wedges of lemon or lime, with fresh crusty bread and a salad, or in a warm, split buttered bun.

EGG-CRUMBED FISH FINGERS

For plenty of crunchy coating, to stop soft-textured fish breaking up, or to make fish go further, cut it into fingers before coating and cooking.

For 2 servings:
200–300g skinless, boneless fish fillets
about ¼ cup flour
½ tsp each celery and garlic salt
1 Tbsp water
1 egg
about ½ cup fine dry breadcrumbs
hot oil for cooking

Cut fish lengthways into fingers about 2cm wide, then cut (diagonally so strips taper at each end) into 8cm lengths. Shake in a plastic bag containing the flour.

Mix flavoured salts with the water, then add the egg and mix with a fork until combined.

Dip floured fish fingers first into the egg mixture, then into the breadcrumbs, and leave on a rack so coating becomes firm.

Cook in hot oil, about 5mm deep, until coating is golden brown, turning once.

Serve with potatoes and green beans, on rice with sweet and sour sauce, or in a hamburger bun with lettuce and tomato.

FISH BATTERCAKES

It's hard to stop thin batter falling off shallow-fried fish. Instead, mix a thicker batter and stir in cubed raw fish. Cook spoonfuls of it.

For 4 servings:
500g boneless, skinless fish fillets
1 egg
¼ cup milk
½ tsp onion salt
½ tsp paprika
½ tsp curry powder
1 cup self-raising flour
oil

Cut the fish into 1cm cubes.

Place the remaining ingredients except oil in a medium-sized bowl. Do not mix until all ingredients have been added, then stir with a fork until dry ingredients are dampened, but mixture still looks lumpy. Fold the fish through the batter.

Cook spoonfuls in hot oil (5mm deep) over a moderate heat until batter is golden brown. Fish will be cooked when the batter in the centre of the battercakes is cooked.

Variation:
Halve 6–12 oysters and add to the batter with the fish. Replace some milk with oyster liquid.

Serve with lemon wedges or Tartare Sauce (page 115).

SPICY CAJUN GRILLED FISH

A Cajun-style coating gives this grilled fish an interesting colour and flavour.

For 4 servings:
1 Tbsp paprika
¼ tsp chilli powder
2 tsp ground cumin
1 tsp garlic salt
1 tsp oreganum
1 tsp thyme
½ tsp turmeric
1 Tbsp flour
600g boneless, skinless fine-textured fish
    fillets
olive or other oil

Measure all the seasonings and the flour into a dry jar with an airtight top. Shake well to mix.

Cut each fish fillet into two pieces by continuing the cut made (before purchase) to remove the central bones, then cut the larger of these pieces diagonally in half, so you finish up with three evenly sized and shaped pieces of fish from each fillet.

Brush each piece of fish lightly with oil, then turn in the seasoning mixture in a

shallow plate to coat evenly. Place the coated fish pieces close together on a piece of lightly oiled foil, twist up the corners, transfer to a preheated grill tray, and grill until the flesh in the thickest part is milky when tested with a fork, probably 3–5 minutes. (It should not be necessary to turn the fillets if they are put on a hot grill tray.)

Serve fish with wedges of fresh lime or lemon, with a stir-fried vegetable mixture over noodles, and Garlic Bread (page 112).

29

▲ *Fish Fillets in Lemon and Caper Sauce*

FISH FILLETS IN LEMON AND CAPER SAUCE

*When fish fillets are turned in a caper sauce thickened with mustard,
they have a lovely tangy flavour.*

For 2 servings:

300–350g boneless, skinless fillets of
    medium-textured fish
¼ cup flour
1 Tbsp butter
1 Tbsp olive or other oil
2 cloves garlic, chopped
¼ cup white wine
1 Tbsp lemon juice
1 Tbsp each capers and caper liquid
pinch of salt
freshly ground black pepper
2 tsp Dijon mustard
1 Tbsp finely chopped parsley

Cut large fillets diagonally into even-
sized pieces if necessary, so that you
finish up with two or three pieces of
almost equal size from each fillet.
Lightly coat by turning in flour, patting it
onto the surface so each piece is evenly
covered.

Melt the butter with the oil in a large
frypan and cook the garlic for about 1
minute. Remove the garlic, and put half
the fish pieces into the hot garlicky oil.
Cook the fish until lightly browned,
about 1 minute on each side. Lift out
and keep warm. Repeat with remaining
fish pieces, then make the sauce.

To the drippings in the pan add the
wine, lemon juice, capers and their
liquid, the seasonings and mustard, and
boil until reduced slightly. Return the
cooked fillets to the pan, turn in the
sauce, and sprinkle with parsley.

*Serve with sautéed potato pieces, and
Savoury Beans and Tomatoes (page 78).*

30

OVEN-FRIED FISH FILLETS

This is the 'fried' fish that I always cook when I do not want my house to smell like
a fish and chip shop, long after the meal is eaten.

For 4 servings:
4 skinless, boneless fish fillets (600g)
¼ cup milk
1 tsp salt or flavoured salt
few drops Tabasco sauce (optional)
½ cup dry breadcrumbs
25–50g butter

Cut fish into serving-sized pieces if necessary.

Mix the milk, salt and Tabasco sauce together in a small bowl. Measure the crumbs onto a shallow plate or paper towel. Coat the fillets first with seasoned milk, then with crumbs.

Preheat oven to 230°C.

Select a shallow baking dish (preferably metal, with a non-stick finish) that will hold the fillets in one layer, and melt the butter in it until it is bubbling but has not burnt.

Turn each fillets in the hot pan so that the side coated first is uppermost. Arrange fillets so they are not touching.

Bake at 230°C for 10–15 minutes, until the flesh in the centre of each fillet flakes, and until the coating has browned in parts. Take care not to overcook or the fish will be dry.

Variation:
Replace about half the breadcrumbs with parmesan cheese for extra flavour and colour.

Serve immediately, with chips or jacket wedges, or Mediterranean Potatoes (page 83), or slip the cooked fish into a heated split bun.

ROSY FISH FILLETS

Easy enough to prepare after work, tasty enough to serve to someone special, and
less than 5 minutes' cooking time!

For 2 servings:
250g boneless skinless fish fillets
2 Tbsp flour
1 tsp ground cumin
1 tsp oreganum
½ tsp garlic salt
½ tsp paprika
about 1 Tbsp oil
½ cup white wine
1 Tbsp tomato paste
2 Tbsp cream

Cut fillets diagonally into 4–6 even-sized pieces. Mix next five ingredients together and coat fish with this mixture. Pan-fry coated fish in a little preheated oil until barely cooked. Remove from pan, pour off any extra oil, then add wine and tomato paste and boil down to half original volume. Stir in cream, replace fish in pan, and turn to coat with sauce.

Serve straight away, with fresh asparagus and new potatoes or Bread Rolls (page 104) or Garlic Bread (page 112) and a green salad.

MARINERS' MUSSELS

This is an interesting and inexpensive fish meal that is also rich in iron!

For 4 servings:
2 large onions
2 cloves garlic
1 Tbsp oil
pinch saffron (optional)
½ cup white wine
425g can whole tomatoes
1½ kg (about 24) fresh mussels
¼ cup chopped parsley

In a large pan with a lid, cook chopped onions and garlic in oil until transparent. Add saffron if available, then add wine and roughly chopped tomatoes and boil for 2 minutes.

Add half the mussels and simmer with the lid on until the shells open about 1cm. Arrange opened mussels in two individual serving bowls, keep warm, and cook the remaining mussels the same way.

Boil the broth briskly for about 2 minutes, then spoon evenly over mussels in bowls. Sprinkle with chopped parsley.

Serve immediately with large amounts of french bread or Garlic Bread (page 112) to dip in the broth.

CREAMY PAPRIKA FISH

This recipe has been one of our favourites for more than twenty years.

For 4 servings:
2 medium-sized onions
25g butter
2 tsp paprika
2 Tbsp flour
1/2 tsp salt
1/2 cup milk
1/2 cup cream, sour cream or evaporated
  milk
750g firm-fleshed, boneless, skinless fish
  fillets, cubed
2 Tbsp chopped parsley

Cut peeled, halved onions lengthways then crossways into quarters and cook gently in butter in a covered pan until tender.

Stir in paprika, cook for 30 seconds longer then add flour and salt. Add the milk and bring to the boil, stirring constantly, then add the cream, sour cream or evaporated milk and bring to the boil again, still stirring.

Cut the fish into 2cm squares about 1cm thick. Gently stir the fish and parsley

into the sauce, cover again, and cook very gently, for 3–5 minutes, until fish is cooked. Taste and adjust seasonings if necessary.

Serve spooned over pasta, or pile on toasted, buttered split rolls and accompany with a salad.

CREOLE FISH

This fish is simmered in a tasty sauce. It is best to use firm-fleshed fish.

For 4 servings:
2 Tbsp butter
2 cloves garlic, chopped
1 green pepper, chopped
1 tsp oreganum
1 tsp ground cumin
1/2 tsp thyme
2 Tbsp flour
425g can Chunky Tomato and Onion
1/2–1 tsp Tabasco sauce
500g fish fillets

Melt the butter in a large pan, add garlic, green pepper and the seasonings, then cook gently for 3–5 minutes.

Stir in the flour, then add the tomatoes and bring to the boil, stirring constantly. Add the Tabasco sauce to taste, then stir in the fish cut into 15cm cubes. Cover the pan and simmer for 3–5 minutes, until fish is just cooked.

Variation:
Replace all or part of the fish with fresh shrimps or prawns.

Serve on rice with a leafy green or other salad (pages 84–87).

FISH VERACRUZ

A few dried chillies and some coriander leaves give this simple Mexican recipe a delicious spicy flavour.

For 3–4 servings:
1 medium-sized onion, sliced
2 or 3 cloves garlic, chopped
2 Tbsp oil
2 dried red chillies, deseeded and sliced*
1 green pepper, chopped
2 bay leaves
1 tsp cumin (optional)
1/2 tsp each oreganum and salt
400g can whole tomatoes
500g firm-fleshed fish fillets, cubed
1–2 tsp minced coriander leaves
1 Tbsp lime (or lemon) juice

Look for dried red chillies 5–7.5cm long. They tend to be less hot than the tiny red ones.

Cook the onion and garlic in the oil, in a large frypan. As soon as the onion softens, add the sliced, deseeded chillies, the green pepper and the bay leaves.

Continue to cook, stirring occasionally, until the onion is translucent and the green pepper is soft, then add the cumin, oreganum and salt. Drain the tomatoes, reserving the juice, then crush the whole tomatoes and add them to the pan with about half the juice.

Gently stir in the cubed fish and simmer gently, stirring once or twice to turn all the fish pieces, for about 5 minutes.

Remove from the heat as soon as the largest cubes of fish are just cooked, and stir in the coriander and lime or lemon juice.

Serve immediately on rice, with a Mixed Green Salad (page 86).

COCONUT FISH CURRY

Select fish with a medium-to-firm texture for this dish.

For 4 servings:
25g butter
2 onions, sliced
2 cloves garlic, chopped
2 tsp curry powder
420g can coconut cream
600–700g fish fillets
¼–½ tsp salt

Melt the butter in a large pan and add the onion and garlic. Cover and cook over a low heat until tender but not browned.

Stir in the curry powder and cook for 1 minute longer over a medium heat then add the coconut cream. Cook uncovered for 5–10 minutes until sauce thickens.

Cut the fish fillets into pieces about 10cm long, up to 4cm wide. Turn pieces in sauce, pack into the pan, preferably in one layer. Cover and simmer until centre of fish is opaque and fish will flake easily, 5–10 minutes. Add salt to taste.

Serve on rice or noodles with a salad or Curry Accompaniments (pages 90–91).

GRILLED SALMON STEAKS

Salmon needs no complicated recipes since it has a lovely flavour of its own, and a pleasing texture.

For 4 servings:
4 salmon steaks (100–150g each)
about 25g butter, melted
2 tsp light soya sauce
2 tsp lemon or lime juice
about ¼ tsp Tabasco sauce

Stand the steaks in one layer on a piece of unpunctured aluminium foil that has had its edges folded over, turned up, and twisted at the corners.

Melt the butter and stir in the soya sauce, lemon or lime juice and Tabasco sauce. Brush the fish with this, covering all surfaces. Cover and refrigerate it if you are not going to cook the fish straight away, then bring to room temperature before you cook it.

Preheat the grill, at the same time heating a solid tray on which the fish will cook. (If your grill has racks only, heat the removable base of a cake tin or something similar.)

Slide the foil container holding the fish onto the preheated surface. (This will ensure that the bottom part of the fish cooks, and you will not need to turn the pieces over.) Grill until the salmon loses its translucency, until it feels firm rather than spongy when you press it, and until the flesh flakes when a small fork or sharp knife is twisted in the thickest part. This may happen in about a minute with a fairly thin steak or fillet under a really hot grill.

Serve on warmed plate, with Hollandaise Sauce (page 115) to which any juices from the foil have been added, and lightly cooked young vegetables.

POACHED SALMON WITH SPINACH AND HOLLANDAISE ON PASTA

This recipe looks particularly attractive when made with fresh salmon, but you can actually use any firm-fleshed fish in its place.

For 2–3 servings:
Hollandaise Sauce
200–300g salmon (or other firm-fleshed fish)
½–1 cup water
½ cup white wine (or 2 Tbsp lemon juice)
2 cloves garlic
1 Tbsp capers
1 tsp peppercorns
fresh herbs (dill, thyme, parsley)
300–400g fresh pasta
100–150g spinach
1–2 Tbsp butter

Make once the recipe of Hollandaise Sauce on page 115, using the larger amount of lemon juice.

Place the boned, skinned fish fillets in a pan with the water, wine or lemon juice and seasonings. Heat gently until just boiling, then turn the fish over and turn off the heat, but leave pan to sit on the hot element until the fish is cooked (when the flesh is opaque to the centre). Drain liquid from the pan and break fish into several smaller pieces, using two forks.

Cook the pasta in boiling water until just tender. Steam (washed) spinach leaves over the pasta as it cooks. Drain pasta and toss in butter.

Arrange pasta on individual plates or a platter, cover with a layer of spinach, then top with the fish pieces. Spoon sauce over this.

Serve a light salad and Bread Rolls (page 104).

SPICY FISH CAKES

These little fish patties have a deliciously Oriental flavour and are quickly mixed and cooked.

For 4 main or 6 starter servings:
500g fish fillets
1 small onion, chopped
1 egg
2 tsp salt
1–2 tsp green curry paste*
1 tsp sesame oil
2 Tbsp chopped coriander leaves
3 slices day-old bread
1 cup water
1 Tbsp lemon juice

*Vary the amount, depending on strength of flavour and hotness desired.

Cut the skinned and boned fillets into 1–2cm cubes. Put into a food processor bowl and process with the chopped onion, egg, salt, curry paste, sesame oil, and coriander until finely minced.

Break the bread into small pieces, removing crusts if a light-coloured mixture is required. Arrange evenly over minced fish mixture.

Dribble three-quarters of the water and the lemon juice over the bread. Process until smooth, adding extra water if

needed. Shape into 16 patties with wet hands.

Heat a non-stick pan with enough oil to cover the surface. When hot add patties and cook over high heat for 2–3 minutes per side, until lightly browned.

Serve hot or warm with lemon or lime wedges. Add rice and other Oriental-style salads or vegetables for a more substantial meal.

◀ *Grilled Salmon Steaks*

PAELLA

This recipe may stray a little from the traditional Spanish version,
but it is still delicious.

For 2–3 large servings:
1 medium-sized onion
2 or 3 cloves of garlic
3 Tbsp oil
1 green and/or red pepper, sliced
¾ cup long-grain white rice
½ tsp each paprika, chilli powder and
    turmeric (or saffron strands)
2 cups hot chicken or fish stock (or 2
    cups water plus 2 tsp instant stock)
2 tomatoes
extra oil
4 chicken wings or drumsticks
200g firm-fleshed fish fillets, cubed, or
    cooked (peeled) shrimps
1 cup frozen peas or beans
4–6 small whole fresh mussels
2 Tbsp chopped parsley

Chop the onion and garlic and cook in the oil in a large pot, pan or wok, until softened and slightly browned, stirring occasionally.

Stir in the sliced pepper and cook for 1–2 minutes, then add the rice. Mix well to ensure all the rice is covered with oil. Stir frequently until the rice looks milky white, then add the spices, stock and cubed tomato. Cover and bring to the boil.

In another pan, in a little extra oil, brown the chicken pieces on all sides, then add to the rice mixture. Simmer for about 15 minutes until the chicken and rice are cooked, stirring occasionally so the rice doesn't stick.

Add the cubed fish, or peeled shrimps, and the peas or beans, stir, then top with the mussels. Replace the lid and cook until the mussels open and the fish is opaque, about 3–5 minutes.

Variation:
Make using only fish and shellfish or with more chicken and no seafood.

Note:
Paella does not reheat well.

Serve immediately sprinkled with parsley.

SMOKED SALMON & MUSHROOM LASAGNE

This is a very elegant and, better still, very easy main dish for dinner parties or special occasions. It also makes a small quantity of smoked salmon go a long way!

For 4 servings:
3 Tbsp butter
3 Tbsp flour
1 tsp garlic salt
¼ tsp grated nutmeg
2½ cups milk
2 cups grated cheese
200g button mushrooms
100–200g smoked salmon
about 150g fresh spinach lasagne sheets
paprika to garnish

Melt the butter in a large pot. Stir in the flour and cook, stirring frequently, for 1–2 minutes. Stir in the garlic salt and nutmeg, then add half the milk.

Whisk or stir vigorously until the mixture thickens and boils. Cook for 1–2 minutes, stirring frequently, then add the remaining milk, again stirring until the mixture boils. Remove from the heat and stir in about three-quarters of the grated cheese.

Finely slice the mushrooms and smoked salmon. Butter or oil a shallow casserole or lasagne dish. Cover the bottom with a single layer of lasagne, then spread half the sliced mushrooms and the

salmon on it. Cover with a third of the sauce, then another layer of lasagne.

Repeat the mushroom and salmon, sauce and lasagne layers, then top with the remaining sauce.

Sprinkle with the rest of the grated cheese and a little paprika, then bake, loosely covered, for 30 minutes at 175°C, then uncovered for a further 15–20 minutes until the top is brown.

If you like, you can make the whole thing ahead and reheat, covered (about 30 minutes, or until the centre is warm, at 175°C) when required.

Serve with a Mixed Green Salad (page 86) and Bread Rolls (page 104).

FILO FISH ROLL

Soft-textured, mild-flavoured fish are rolled in sheets of filo, sponge-roll style.
Baked then sliced, the roll has an interesting texture and a good flavour.

For 4 servings:
400–500g fish fillets
6 sheets filo pastry
melted butter or oil for brushing
½ cup sour cream
4 spring onions, finely chopped
1–2 cups sliced mushrooms or 1 cup
    chopped peppers
fresh herbs, e.g. dill, parsley
garlic salt

Slice the fish fillets into fairly thin diagonal slices.

Brush three sheets of filo pastry with melted butter or oil. Place side by side, slightly overlapping (long sides together). Cover with three more sheets. Spread with sour cream then place the fish over this.

Add spring onion and mushroom, or pepper and herbs. Sprinkle with garlic

salt and roll up. Brush with a little more melted butter or oil.

Bake at 190°C for about 40 minutes. Allow to stand for 15 minutes before serving.

Serve with a salad (pages 84–87) or baby spring vegetables.

Paella ▶

▲ *Easy Fish Fillets*

THAI-STYLE SQUID WITH VEGETABLES

This spicy, Thai-inspired dish is really very simple. The sauce is also delicious with chicken or even with vegetables alone.

For 2–3 servings:
2 squid tubes (about 180g)
1 Tbsp each sesame oil and light soya
    sauce
2 cloves garlic
1cm fresh ginger, grated
1 small onion
1 green pepper
2 cups broccoli florets
1 cup button mushrooms
1 Tbsp each Thai fish sauce, oyster sauce
    and dark soya sauce
1 tsp sugar
1–2 Tbsp chopped coriander leaves
2 Tbsp oil
½–1 tsp red curry paste (optional)
1 dried red chilli (optional)
chopped coriander or spring onions to
    garnish

Halve the squid tubes lengthways, trim and discard any remaining cartilage. Lay each half flat on a board with the inside facing upwards. With a sharp knife, score the surface into 1cm diamond shapes. Cut into rectangles about 2 x 4cm. Place scored squid in a bowl and toss with the sesame oil, soya sauce, garlic and ginger. Allow to stand.

Halve and slice the onion and green pepper, cut the broccoli into bite-sized pieces and slice the mushrooms.

Measure the fish, oyster and soya sauces, sugar and coriander into a small bowl. Heat the oil in large wok or frypan. Add the onion (and curry paste

and sliced, deseeded chilli if desired), stir for about 1 minute, then add the broccoli, green pepper and mushrooms. Cook, stirring occasionally, until the broccoli is barely tender.

Add the squid and cook for 2–3 minutes, stirring frequently, then add the sauce mixture, toss, and remove from the heat. It is important not to overcook the squid or it will become chewy and tough.

Serve immediately over fragrant Thai (jasmine) rice. Garnish with chopped coriander or spring onions.

38

EASY FISH FILLETS

This is a very quick and easy way to cook fish. You can cook it either in a microwave oven or a conventional oven.

For 4 servings:
1½ Tbsp butter
4 skinless, boneless fish fillets (400–600g)
1 tsp garlic salt
½ tsp paprika
2 Tbsp chopped parsley or other fresh herbs

Melt the butter in a dish large enough to hold the fillets in one layer. Turn the fillets in the melted butter.

Arrange fish with the thicker parts towards the edge. Sprinkle with garlic salt, paprika and parsley, using more or less seasoning according to taste.

To microwave:
Cover tightly with plastic cling film without leaving air vents and cook for 4–5 minutes on High (100% power), until the fish is opaque in the thickest parts. Allow to stand for 2–3 minutes before uncovering. (During this time the film should press the seasonings onto the fish.)

To bake conventionally:
Bake uncovered at 200°C for 10–20 minutes, depending on the thickness of the fish. Take care not to overcook — the fish is ready as soon as it is milky white in its thickest part.

Serve with a Mixed Green Salad (page 86) and Bread Rolls (page 104).

MUSSELS IN CURRIED TOMATO SAUCE

This recipe is best made with small fresh green-lipped mussels, often sold live in larger supermarkets.

For 2–3 servings:
½ cup dry white wine
½ cup water
1 onion, finely chopped
2 cloves garlic, finely chopped
thyme, dill, fennel or parsley
12 mussels in the shell
1 Tbsp butter
½ tsp curry powder
1 Tbsp flour
½ cup tomato juice
2 Tbsp cream
½ cup peeled, chopped tomato

Combine the wine, water, onion and garlic in a large frypan. Simmer gently while chopping any or all of the fresh herbs mentioned. If fresh herbs are not available, use dried herbs in amounts to suit your taste. Put mussels in the simmering liquid, cover, and cook until the shells open wide, then remove. Take the mussels out of their shells, discarding beards etc.

Strain the cooking liquid into a bowl and discard vegetables.

Melt the butter in the pan, add the curry powder and cook gently for about a minute, stir in the flour, tomato juice and the strained cooking liquid. Stir until smooth and thick, then add the cream. Bring back to the boil, add the cooked mussels and the pieces of tomato and heat through. Do not leave the mixture simmering, or the mussels will shrink and toughen. Taste, adjust seasoning if necessary, and sprinkle with more of any fresh herb used earlier.

Serve with Bread Rolls (page 104), on pasta, or with rice with a leafy green salad on the side.

BAKED FISH WITH LEMON AND HORSERADISH SAUCE

Lemon and horseradish combine well to form a delicious and unusual sauce for this easy baked fish. Use any reasonably firm type of fish. Ask for advice about fish textures in the store if you are unsure.

For 3–4 servings:
2 Tbsp butter
2 Tbsp flour
1 cup milk
½ tsp garlic salt
1 Tbsp horseradish sauce
grated rind of 1 lemon (about 1–2 tsp)
2 Tbsp lemon juice
¼ tsp turmeric
½–1 cup grated cheese
400–500g fish fillets
turmeric to garnish

Melt the butter in a medium-sized pot or frypan. Stir in the flour to form a thick paste, and continue to cook, stirring continuously for 2 minutes.

Add about a third of the milk and stir to form a thick, lump-free paste. Allow to boil, then add another third of the milk, and continue stirring until the sauce returns to the boil. Add the final third of the milk and bring to the boil again, stirring to give a smooth sauce.

Remove from the heat and add the next five ingredients, then add half of the grated cheese and stir until well mixed.

Spread half of the sauce over the bottom of a shallow ovenproof dish (about 15 x 25cm). Cut the fish fillets into serving-sized pieces and arrange these in the dish. Pour over the remaining sauce, then top with the remaining grated cheese, and sprinkle with turmeric.

Bake for 15 minutes at 220°C, then grill briefly to brown the top if necessary.

Serve with new potatoes or Pasta Salad (page 81).

TUNA SAUCE ON PASTA

This sauce can easily be prepared while the pasta cooks. It is good in its basic tomato, onion and tuna form, or 'dressed up' with the optional additions.

For 2–3 servings:
250–300g spaghetti or fettucini
1–2 Tbsp olive oil
1 onion, quartered and sliced
2 cloves garlic
1 green pepper, sliced (optional)
400g can tomatoes in juice
1 Tbsp pesto or 1 tsp dried basil
125g can tuna
black pepper
1 Tbsp capers (optional)
3 or 4 anchovy fillets, chopped (optional)
10–12 green or black olives (optional)

Boil the pasta according to the instructions on the packet.

While the pasta cooks, heat the oil in a large frypan, and cook the onion and garlic gently, until the onion begins to turn clear. Add the green pepper (if used) and continue to cook for 1–2 minutes, then add the tomatoes and juice. Crush the tomatoes to break them up into bite-sized pieces.

Add the pesto or basil, then stir well and add the drained tuna. Stir to break up any large lumps, but don't mash.

Simmer gently until well heated, then season to taste with black pepper and add any of the remaining optional ingredients.

Drain the pasta and toss with a little butter or olive oil. Pour sauce over the pasta on individual plates or on a serving platter.

Serve immediately with a salad (pages 84–87) and Garlic Bread (page 112).

SALAD NICOISE

(See photograph pages 26–27.)
This makes a wonderful hot-weather main course. For best appearance, arrange the ingredients, one at a time, on the individual dinner plates.

For 2 servings:
2 eggs
4–6 small new potatoes
100–150g green beans
mixed lettuce leaves, preferably small
2 medium-sized or 8–10 baby tomatoes
10cm length of telegraph cucumber
185–200g can tuna
2–4 spring onions, diagonally sliced
4–6 anchovy fillets, whole or chopped
8–12 black olives

Dressing:
2 Tbsp lemon juice
6 Tbsp olive oil
1 tsp Dijon mustard

At least 30 minutes before serving time hard-boil the eggs and cook the new potatoes and green beans. Cool after cooking. Assemble and prepare the remaining ingredients while these cook.

A short time before serving, make a bed of lettuce leaves on two dinner plates.

Arrange on these the sliced unpeeled potatoes, the eggs, quartered or cut in six wedges, the whole or sliced green beans (depending on size) and the whole or quartered tomatoes. Cut cucumber in half lengthways, scoop out seedy part with a teaspoon, then cut in slices. Arrange with the other

vegetables. Drain and flake the tuna, and place in the centre of the plates. Top with spring onions, anchovy fillets and olives.

Just before serving, shake together dressing ingredients and drizzle over salads.

Serve with french bread or Garlic Bread (page 112).

OLD-FASHIONED FISH PIE

As this fish pie contains potatoes and leeks, you need serve nothing else with it to have a satisfying, well-balanced main course.

For 4 servings:
2 leeks (about 600g)
2 tsp butter
¼ cup water
310g can smoked fish fillets
2 eggs, hard-boiled
1½ cups reserved liquid (see below)
milk
2 Tbsp butter
½ tsp curry powder
2 Tbsp flour
750g potatoes, cooked and mashed
2 Tbsp grated parmesan cheese

Cut the washed leeks into 1cm slices, cook with 2 tsp butter and ¼ cup water, covered, for about 5 minutes, and drain, reserving liquid.

Drain the fish and reserve liquid, break fish into chunks and put into a lightly buttered or sprayed casserole dish, about 18 x 23cm. Spread the leeks over the fish, and add the hard-boiled eggs, chopped into pieces.

Put reserved fish and leek cooking liquids into a measuring cup, and make up to 1½ cups with milk. Melt the butter with the curry powder, add the flour, and heat until it bubbles. Stir the liquid

in gradually, bringing to the boil between each addition, and simmer for 5 minutes. Pour over the fish, leeks, and eggs.

Spoon prepared mashed potato over fish and sauce mixture, sprinkle top with the parmesan cheese. Heat uncovered at about 175°C, until potato topping is lightly browned and crisp and bottom is bubbling, about 20 minutes.

Serve alone (as it contains potatoes and leeks as well as fish) or with a Spinach Salad (page 86).

Kedgeree ▲

KEDGEREE

Kedgeree is an interesting mixture of smoked fish, curry and rice. For maximum flavour, eat this mixture soon after the fish is mixed with the rice.

For 4–5 servings:

1 Tbsp butter
1 large clove garlic, sliced
¼ cup white wine
freshly ground black pepper
600–700g smoked fish fillets
2 Tbsp butter
2 onions, finely chopped
1 tsp curry powder
½ tsp turmeric
1 cup basmati rice
2¼ cups liquid (reserved fish stock made up to this quantity with water)
3 eggs, hard-boiled, chopped
1 Tbsp lemon juice
fresh dill and parsley, chopped
3 spring onions, chopped
salt and pepper (optional)
wedges of lemon to garnish

Heat the first measure of butter in a large frypan, cook the garlic for a few minutes, then add the wine, pepper, and fish fillets. Cover and poach the fillets for 5–7 minutes, or until the fish flakes easily, turning once after 4–5 minutes.

Drain the liquid from the fish through a sieve and put it aside. Flake the fish, removing and discarding skin and bones.

Melt the second measure of butter in a pot, add the onions and cook until soft but not browned. Add the curry powder and turmeric and cook, stirring constantly for about a minute. Add the uncooked rice and the reserved fish stock made up to 2¼ cups with water.

Cover and cook over low heat for 10–15 minutes, until the rice is tender and the liquid absorbed. Remove from the heat, and fold the flaked fish, hard-boiled eggs, lemon juice and the herbs through the rice. Season with salt and pepper if necessary.

Variation:

Use canned smoked fish fillets instead of freshly smoked fish.

To serve, sprinkle with the chopped spring onions. Garnish with wedges of lemon.

Chicken Mains

Chicken plays a very important part in a semi-vegetarian eating pattern, and may be eaten four or five times a week. For variety and interest it is important to have a wide repertoire of chicken recipes.

In the following chapter, the largest in this book, you will find chicken cooked in many different ways. In some recipes the flavour of the chicken itself predominates, and in others, strongly flavoured ingredients are used with the chicken. This contrast is intended, and is especially helpful for the person who has recently decided to stop eating red meat, and misses some strong meat flavours.

When you cook chicken often, make sure it doesn't always look the same. Choose recipes calling for whole chicken, bone-in joints, the larger boneless skinless cuts, and small slices and cubes, instead of always using only one or two of these.

Make sure that you are aware of new chicken (and turkey) products on the market. In the rapidly growing poultry industry, these appear often.

Don't throw out bones, giblets and trimmings which you can boil up for stock. Remember that chicken livers are an excellent source of iron (an important mineral in our diet) as well as being excellent value for money.

◀ *Roasted Chicken Legs and Summer Vegetables (page 57)*

▲ *Stir-Fried Chicken*

STIR-FRIED CHICKEN

When tender chicken breast meat is cut into thin strips it cooks very quickly.
Teamed with tender-crisp colourful vegetables, it tastes as good as it looks.

For 2 servings:

about 200g chicken breast meat
1 tsp grated root ginger
1 clove garlic, sliced
1 Tbsp light soya sauce
1 Tbsp sherry
1 tsp brown sugar
1 tsp instant chicken stock
1 tsp cornflour
2 Tbsp oil
2–3 cups prepared vegetables*
1–2 Tbsp water

*Choose a selection of quick-cooking
vegetables, e.g. spinach, mushrooms,
celery, spring onions, green and red
peppers. Slice the vegetables into pieces
about the same size as the chicken.

Cut the chicken breast meat across the
grain into 5mm thick slices. Put into a
plastic bag with the next seven
ingredients. Knead bag lightly to
combine thoroughly, allow to stand for
at least 15 minutes.

Heat the oil in a large frypan over a
very high heat. Add the prepared
vegetables and toss until coated with oil
and heated through. Add 1–2
tablespoons water, cover and cook until
the vegetables are barely tender, then
remove from pan. Add a little extra oil if
necessary, then stir in the chicken. Stir
over a very high heat until chicken
strips turn white, then return vegetables
to the pan. Toss gently to mix.

*Serve straight after cooking, on noodles
or rice (page 90).*

TWO-MINUTE CHICKEN BREASTS

This is a wonderfully quick recipe to make when you rush into the house after work, without the energy to make anything elaborate or time-consuming.

For 2 servings:
*3 chicken breasts
1 Tbsp sherry
2 tsp sesame oil
2 tsp brown sugar
1 clove garlic, finely chopped
$\frac{1}{2}$ tsp grated root ginger
1–2 Tbsp oil
1 tsp cornflour
1 Tbsp sherry
1 Tbsp water
chives, spring onions or coriander leaves*

Cut each chicken breast into six or nine pieces.

Mix together the first measure of sherry, the sesame oil, brown sugar, garlic and root ginger. Marinate the chicken pieces in this mixture for at least 5 minutes but preferably longer. (Refrigerate the chicken, in its marinade, in a plastic bag, if you like to work ahead, and want an instant meal without any last-minute chopping or grating.)

Heat the oil in a heavy non-stick pan, add the marinated chicken and the liquid around it, and stir-fry for about 2 minutes, or until the chicken flesh is opaque right through.

Mix the cornflour, extra sherry and water, pour over the chicken and toss to coat with the lightly thickened liquid. Serve immediately, sprinkled with chopped chives, spring onion, or fresh coriander leaves.

Serve with Bread Rolls (page 104) and a salad (pages 84–87), or on rice (page 90) or noodles.

PEANUT AND PASTA SALAD WITH CHICKEN

You may think this is a strange recipe, but we think you will enjoy it. Try it as an interesting addition to a buffet for a number of people.

200–300g fresh vegetables
250g ribbon pasta
sesame oil
$\frac{1}{4}$ cup crunchy peanut butter
2 cloves garlic, chopped
2 Tbsp light soya sauce
2 Tbsp wine vinegar
1 Tbsp soft brown sugar
1 Tbsp sesame oil
Tabasco sauce to taste
3 cooked chicken breasts
$\frac{1}{2}$ cup chopped roasted peanuts
2 spring onions, diagonally sliced*

*Select a mixture, e.g. carrots, green beans, celery.

Cut the vegetables into matchstick strips, mix them and cook in a small amount of lightly salted water for 4–5 minutes, or until tender-crisp. Do not overcook.

Cook the pasta in a large potful of lightly salted boiling water, until just tender. Drain, rinse with cold water, and add about a teaspoon of sesame or plain oil. Add more oil if you are leaving the pasta to stand for long.

While the pasta and vegetables cook, mix the next six ingredients in a food processor, then thin down to pouring cream consistency with about $\frac{1}{4}$ cup of boiling water. Add Tabasco sauce to taste. Cut the chicken into long thin strips.

To assemble the salad: Mix the pasta with about half the sauce. Toss the drained vegetables with a little more of the sauce, and arrange them on the pasta. Arrange the chicken on top of the vegetables, then drizzle the remaining sauce over it. Sprinkle with the peanuts and spring onions.

Serve soon after assembling, at room temperature.

GRILLED CHICKEN BREASTS

These chicken breasts are good served alone, with apricot sauce or with a little Sun-Dried Tomato Paste spread over them, or spread on the fresh crusty bread served with them.

For 4 servings:
*2 chicken breasts
1 Tbsp olive oil
1 Tbsp light soya sauce
1 Tbsp sweet chilli sauce*

Put one boneless, skinless chicken breast between two sheets of plastic. Using a rolling pin, bang evenly and gently until the breast is of even thickness and double its original length and width. Repeat with the second breast.

Combine oil, soya sauce and chilli sauce, and brush over the chicken.

Grill or barbecue for about 5 minutes each side or until cooked through.

(Take care not to overcook.)

Serve sliced with Bread Rolls (page 104), Tomato Salsa (page 114) or Sun-Dried Tomato Paste (page 113).

FILO CHICKEN PARCELS

Filo parcels always look attractive. They may be prepared ahead and cooked later, or cooked straight away and reheated later.

For 2 servings:

2 small boneless, skinless chicken
    breasts, cooked and cut into 1cm
    cubes
4–6 mushrooms, sliced
1 Tbsp olive oil
2 Tbsp white wine
1 Tbsp finely chopped parsley
2 tsp fresh thyme, finely chopped
4 sheets filo pastry
2 tsp butter, melted
slices Brie or Camembert, cubed
oil for brushing pastry

Brown the chicken cubes lightly with the mushrooms in the oil for about 1 minute. Add the wine and herbs and cook for 1 minute longer, until liquid has evaporated. Leave to cool.

Brush two sheets of filo lightly with melted butter, cover with remaining filo.

Place half the chicken mixture with half the cheese on each double sheet. Wrap up loosely in the same style as you would wrap a parcel.

Place parcels join-side down in a shallow oven tray and brush lightly with oil. Bake at 180°C for 12–15 minutes, until filo is evenly golden brown.

Serve immediately or reheat at the same temperature when required. Good with Eggplants with Parsley and Garlic (page 78) or Savoury Beans and Tomatoes (page 78).

QUICK CHICKEN SATAY STICKS

This is a good way to turn a couple of chicken breasts into a quick, interesting meal.

For 2 servings:

2 boneless, skinless chicken breasts
1–2 Tbsp lemon or lime juice
1 Tbsp each soya sauce and fish sauce
1–2 tsp sesame oil
1 tsp ground cumin
2 cloves garlic, finely chopped
1 tsp grated fresh ginger
1 Tbsp chopped coriander leaves
    (optional)
1 cup satay sauce, bought or homemade

Soak 12 bamboo skewers in cold water.

Cut the chicken breasts lengthways into 1cm strips. Place strips in a bag with all the remaining ingredients, except the satay sauce.

Leave to marinate from 5 minutes to 24 hours, as time allows. Thread the chicken strips lengthways onto the skewers and grill or barbecue close to the heat until cooked, 3–5 minutes each side (juice should run clear when chicken is pierced).

Serve on rice with warm satay sauce and a cucumber or other salad (pages 84–87).

MEXICAN CHICKEN

This tasty and popular chicken is very easy to make using a homemade seasoning mix.

For 4 servings:

6–8 boneless, skinless chicken thighs or
    4 chicken breasts
1 tsp each oil and butter
2 Tbsp Mexican Coating Mixture (page
    114)

Make sure all skin and bone is removed from chicken.

Bang chicken breasts between two pieces of plastic, using a rolling pin, until they are 1cm thick. Make sure that thighs will lie flat, snipping meat if necessary. Brush with, or turn in, a mixture of melted butter and oil.

Sprinkle the chicken on both sides with Mexican seasoning, using quantities to suit your taste (about a teaspoon per side for each piece gives a good flavour).

Grill or barbecue close to the heat, until juices no longer run pink, or microwave pieces in one layer in a covered dish, to the same stage, allowing about 1$\frac{1}{2}$ minutes on Medium (50% power) per thigh, and 2 minutes per breast.

Serve with Barbecued Fresh Vegetables (page 80) or Roasted Pepper Salad (page 81) or cool and shred for use in tacos, burritos, etc.

FLORENTINE CHICKEN

*For this recipe you can work ahead — the coated, uncooked chicken may be kept
for 24 hours in the refrigerator before cooking.*

For 2 servings:
2 boneless, skinless chicken breasts
2 Tbsp grated parmesan cheese
2 Tbsp dry breadcrumbs
1 tsp chopped fresh herbs
milk
1 Tbsp oil
1 Tbsp butter

Put one boneless, skinless chicken
breast between two sheets of plastic.
Using a rolling pin, bang evenly and
gently until the breast is of even
thickness and double its original length
and width. Repeat with the second
breast.

Mix together the parmesan cheese,
breadcrumbs and herbs. Dip each piece
first in milk, then in the cheese mixture.
Refrigerate between plastic until
required.

Heat the oil and butter in a large frypan
and cook the chicken over a high heat
for about 1 minute a side, until coating
is golden.

*Serve immediately with two or more
vegetables (one with a sauce). Try
Vegetables à la Grecque (page 79).*

47

▲ *Balti Chicken Curry*

QUICK CHICKEN BIRYANI

This recipe is a mixture of a curry sauce, rice and chicken. Traditionally, everything is cooked together, but here the components are prepared individually, then combined.

For 3–4 servings:
1 cup basmati rice
Mild Curry Sauce
1 Tbsp oil
½ tsp chilli powder
5 whole cloves (optional)
2 whole cardamoms, crushed (optional)
2.5cm piece cinnamon stick (optional)
1 star anise 'flower' (optional)
300g boneless, skinless chicken breasts or thighs, cubed
½ cup unsweetened yoghurt
½ tsp salt
1 tsp garam masala
1 tsp oil
¼–½ cup whole or chopped almonds
¼–½ cup raisins, sultanas or currants

Cook the rice (page 90). Prepare once the recipe of Mild Curry Sauce (page 114).

Heat the first measure of oil in a frypan and add the chilli powder and whole spices (if used). Stir-fry for about a minute, then add the chicken and stir-fry for about a minute longer.

Add the curry sauce to the pan and simmer gently, stirring occasionally for 5–10 minutes or until the pieces of chicken are cooked. Add the yoghurt, salt and garam masala and simmer for a few minutes longer. Remove from the heat, then combine the chicken and rice mixtures.

Heat the remaining oil in a small frypan, add the almonds and stir until these have darkened in colour and smell toasted. Add the dried fruit, then remove from the heat and combine with the chicken and rice.

Serve with a selection of your favourite chutneys, condiments, and poppadoms or other Indian breads (pages 90–91).

BALTI CHICKEN CURRY

This style of curry is cooked very quickly in a heavy frypan or wok, using tender chicken cuts that need very little cooking.

For 2 servings:
300g boneless, skinless chicken breasts or
    thighs
1–2 Tbsp oil
2 cloves garlic, finely chopped
1 large onion, finely chopped
1–2 Tbsp curry paste*
½ cup chicken stock or water
1–2 tsp garam masala
1 Tbsp chopped fresh coriander leaves
salt to taste

*Use bought curry paste or make your
own (page 114).

Cut the chicken into long strips about 1cm thick. In a wok or large frypan, heat the oil over a medium heat and cook garlic very briefly (about 30 seconds). Add the onion and cook until lightly and evenly browned, about 4–5 minutes. Stir in the curry paste, then add the chicken, raise the heat and stir-fry until the chicken loses its raw look, about 3–5 minutes.

Add the chicken stock or water and simmer, stirring, on a lower heat for 5 minutes. Test a piece of chicken to check that it is cooked right through. If

not, cook for a few minutes longer. Add the garam masala and coriander. Mix to combine well, add salt to taste, and serve immediately.

Serve with rice, poppadoms and your choice of other curry accompaniments (pages 90–91).

THAI GREEN CHICKEN CURRY

Thai cooking does require some special ingredients, but most keep well and once you have them on hand they can be used to produce a variety of quick and delicious meals.

For 3–4 servings:
3 or 4 kaffir lime leaves
2 Tbsp oil
1–2 Tbsp Thai green curry paste
1 cup coconut cream
300–400g boneless, skinless chicken
    thighs or breasts
1 medium-sized onion, sliced
2 Tbsp fish sauce
1 tsp sugar
2 or 3 zucchini, sliced
½ cup peas or green beans, fresh or
    frozen
150–200g can bamboo shoots, drained
    (optional)

Cover the lime leaves with a little boiling water, and put aside to soak for a few minutes.

Meanwhile, heat the oil in a frypan or wok. Stir in the curry paste and cook for 1–2 minutes, then add the lime leaves cut into 1cm slices.

Carefully pour in the coconut cream, and add the chicken pieces, cut into 2cm cubes. Add the onion, fish sauce and sugar and simmer for 5 minutes, stirring occasionally.

Add the vegetables, and bamboo shoots

(if you wish) and ¼–½ cup of water to thin sauce if required. Simmer until chicken is cooked through and vegetables are just tender, then serve.

Variation:
For a vegetarian alternative, omit the chicken and add 1–2 cups of assorted vegetables (cubed potato, eggplant, cauliflower, broccoli, etc.) and replace the fish sauce with light soya sauce.

Serve over fragrant Thai (jasmine) rice, garnished with chopped basil or spring onion and curry accompaniments (pages 90–91) of your choice.

THAI RED CHICKEN CURRY

The curry paste, fish sauce, and kaffir lime leaves give many Thai foods their distinctive taste and aroma. If you are hooked on Thai food, it is worth looking for these at specialty Asian food stores.

For 2–3 large servings:
3 kaffir lime leaves or bay leaves
2 Tbsp oil
2–3 Tbsp Thai red curry paste
1 cup coconut cream
300–400g minced chicken
2 Tbsp fish sauce
2 tsp sugar
½ cup roasted peanuts, minced
1 Tbsp chopped coriander leaves
chopped fresh basil and coarsley
    chopped peanuts to garnish

Cover the lime or bay leaves in a little boiling water, and leave to soak for a few minutes.

Heat the oil in a large frypan over a medium heat. Add the curry paste and stir for 1–2 minutes. (Vary the quantity of curry paste to suit your taste — some are very hot.) Carefully mix in about a third of the coconut cream, and when well combined, add the chicken.

Add the remaining coconut cream, the lime leaves, fish sauce and sugar, then the minced or very finely chopped peanuts.

Simmer for 5–10 minutes, stirring occasionally, until the chicken is cooked, then add the chopped coriander leaves.

Serve over fragrant Thai (jasmine) rice, garnished with chopped fresh basil and coarsely chopped peanuts. Choose from the curry accompaniments (pages 90–91).

RED-COOKED CHICKEN

Here is a recipe for barbecued chicken with a difference! The chicken is precooked in a strongly flavoured sauce, before it is barbecued or grilled.

For 4 servings:
4 chicken legs
1 cup cold water
½ cup dark soya sauce
½ cup light soya sauce
2 Tbsp sherry
walnut-sized piece fresh ginger, peeled
    and sliced
1 clove garlic, peeled
1 star anise 'flower'
1½ Tbsp sugar

To microwave:
Combine all the ingredients except the chicken in an unpunctured oven bag then add the chicken legs. Microwave on High (100% power) for 12–14 minutes, or until juices are no longer pink when thighs are pierced deeply, turning pieces in the bag two or three times.

To cook conventionally:
Simmer the chicken legs in the marinade in a covered pan for 15–30 minutes, turning once or twice. Test as above.

Pour off cooking liquid, strain and refrigerate for re-use within a week, or freeze it for later use.

Barbecue or grill the chicken soon after precooking, or refrigerate until required. The chicken can be cooked quite close to the heat, as it is already cooked and needs only reheating.

Serve hot with Barbecued Fresh Vegetables (page 80), warmed Bread Rolls (page 104) and a leafy green salad.

TANDOORI CHICKEN

This popular Indian dish is best prepared ahead and left in its marinade overnight (or at least for 1–2 hours). It cooks with little last-minute fuss.

For 4 servings:
3 or 4 cloves garlic
1–2cm root ginger, grated
½ tsp chilli powder
1 tsp each ground cumin, coriander,
    paprika, turmeric, garam masala
    and mint
1 tsp salt
1 cup unsweetened yoghurt
8 small or 4 large chicken pieces (skin
    removed if you like)

Crush and chop the garlic and grate the ginger. Combine with all of the spices, mint and salt in a shallow container, large enough to hold the chicken pieces in a single layer, or in an unpunctured plastic bag.

Stir in the yoghurt to make a paste. Add the chicken pieces, turning to make sure all are well coated with the spice mixture.

Cover the container and allow to stand for 1–2 hours, or refrigerate overnight if possible.

Arrange chicken pieces on a rack and grill 12–15cm away from the grill or barbecue and cook for 10–20 minutes per side, depending on the thickness. The chicken is cooked when the juices run clear, not pink, when the pieces are pierced.

Serve with plain rice, or Spicy Rice Pilaf (page 82), a salad and your favourite Indian breads.

SESAME CHICKEN

Small bone-in chicken pieces cook in a short time in this sauce, whether microwaved, baked, grilled or barbecued.

For 2 servings:
about 300g chicken wings or drumsticks
2 Tbsp each soya sauce and sherry
1 Tbsp each sugar and sesame oil
1 clove garlic, finely chopped
½ tsp cornflour (if microwaving)
2 Tbsp toasted sesame seeds

To microwave:
Put the prepared chicken pieces in an oven bag, then add all the remaining ingredients except the sesame seed. (Use dark soya sauce for a browner glaze.) Leave for 5 minutes to 24 hours before cooking.

Place bag flat in microwave, with pieces in one layer. Leave a finger-sized opening for steam to escape, and microwave on High (100% power) for about 6 minutes. Flip bag over, stand for about 2 minutes, then pierce the thickest piece. If juice runs pink, cook for longer, in 1-minute bursts, until juices are clear.

Remove from bag and sprinkle with

toasted sesame seeds before glaze sets.

To cook conventionally:
Bag chicken and other ingredients, using dark or light soya sauce, but do not add cornflour. Marinate as above. Fasten bag with a twist tie, leaving a finger-sized hole. Lie bag flat and bake at 180°C for 20–30 minutes, then test and coat with sesame seeds as above.

To barbecue or grill:
Marinate chicken as above but without adding cornflour and sugar. Cook close to heat for about 20 minutes, turning and brushing with remaining marinade. Test as above.

Serve with a salad of your choice (pages 84–87).

Red-cooked Chicken ▲

EASY ORIENTAL SIMMERED CHICKEN

*Here is a very popular and easy recipe, originally from an American
friend with Korean parents.*

For 4–6 servings:
8–12 bone-in chicken pieces
½ cup light soya sauce
1 Tbsp honey
¼ cup sugar
1 cup water
2 Tbsp grated root ginger
2 or 3 cloves garlic, crushed
2 or 3 petals star anise
2 Tbsp sherry
4 spring onions, chopped
cornflour to thicken

Put the pieces of chicken in a pot
(preferably a stovetop-to-table variety)
with all the ingredients except the
spring onion and cornflour.

Bring to the boil then simmer on a very
low heat for 45–60 minutes, or until the
chicken is tender. Add the chopped
spring onions and thicken the liquid as
desired, with cornflour mixed to a paste
with cold water.

*Serve chicken and sauce over rice, with
Wilted Cucumber Salad (page 91).*

51

▲ *Greek Barbecued Chicken*

GREEK BARBECUED CHICKEN

Cooked outdoors on a barbecue, or inside on a grill, this chicken is easy to prepare and cook without fuss.

For 4 servings:
4 large or 8 small bone-in chicken pieces
juice of 1 lemon
¼ cup olive or other oil
1 tsp paprika (optional)
2 cloves garlic, crushed
1 tsp oreganum

Choose chicken legs or quartered chickens for this recipe, or thread wings or small pieces on skewers for easier turning during cooking. If necessary, break joints so pieces lie flat.

Put chicken with all the remaining ingredients in an unpunctured plastic bag. Allow to stand for 30 minutes, turning bag occasionally.

For barbecued chicken:
Cook chicken about 15–20cm from the heat, brushing frequently with marinade.

For grilled chicken:
Lay the chicken pieces in a shallow, foil-lined pan and pour the marinade over to coat well. Grill 15–20cm from the heat, turning pieces several times so they are well cooked.

Chicken is cooked in 20–30 minutes, as soon as juices run clear, not pink, when flesh close to bone is pierced.

Serve hot or at room temperature with a Mediterranean Salad or a Mixed Green Salad (page 86).

PAPRIKA BAKED CHICKEN

This country-style chicken has been one of our favourites for years. It is good hot or cold, indoors or out, and its tasty coating may be made ahead.

For 2 servings:
1 Tbsp butter, melted
1 Tbsp oil
4 chicken drumsticks or thighs
2 Tbsp flour
1 tsp paprika
½ – 1 tsp curry powder
1 tsp garlic salt
1 tsp caster sugar

Melt butter with the oil, and brush over chicken pieces to coat evenly.

Mix remaining dry ingredients together in a screw-topped jar, then transfer most of this mixture to a small sieve and shake it evenly over the chicken pieces, turning them once. Return any unused coating to the jar.

To microwave:
Arrange chicken on a shallow dish so pieces are equidistant from centre of microwave oven, with the thickest parts towards the outside. Microwave covered with a paper towel, on High (100% power) for 8 minutes, turning once after 5 minutes. Test and cook longer if necessary.

To cook conventionally:
Bake in a shallow foil-lined dish at 200°C for 40 minutes, turning after 20 minutes.

Test by piercing in the thickest part, to ensure juices run clear, not pink.

Serve hot with new potatoes or Bread Rolls (page 104) and a salad (pages 84–87), or at room temperature as finger food.

LEMON GARLIC CHICKEN

Make this dish in a shallow oven-to-table dish. The chicken should be arranged in one layer and should just fit the baking dish.

For 4 servings:
4 chicken legs
2 Tbsp butter
2 cloves garlic
¼ tsp dried or 1 tsp fresh chopped tarragon or thyme
2 lemons, rind and juice
water or wine
1 tsp salt
pepper

Put the chicken pieces with best side facing down in the oven dish. Dot with the butter. Slice each clove of garlic into two or three pieces, and place evenly round the dish. Sprinkle the chicken with tarragon or thyme.

Peel several strips of lemon peel from each lemon and place round the chicken. Squeeze the lemon, add water or wine to make up to ½ cup of liquid, and add to the chicken. Sprinkle with salt and pepper, cover tightly with foil

and bake at 200°C for 30 minutes. Remove from the oven, turn the pieces and baste with the juices. Cook uncovered for a further 20 minutes, spooning the liquid over the chicken pieces several times.

Serve immediately, if possible, otherwise cover loosely with the foil and keep warm. Good with Vegetables à la Grecque (page 79), asparagus or broccoli, and new potatoes.

SAUTEED CHICKEN IN WINE

Choose a fresh herb such as thyme, tarragon, marjoram or basil to flavour this easily prepared dish.

For 4 servings:
8 boneless, skinless chicken thighs or drumsticks
¼ cup of flour
2–3 Tbsp butter
1 or 2 cloves garlic, sliced
1 cup dry white wine
½ tsp salt
2 tsp chopped fresh herbs
finely chopped parsley to garnish

Shake the chicken pieces in a plastic bag with the flour. Brown chicken evenly in the butter in a large frypan over a high heat. When browned pour off any extra butter and turn down heat. Add garlic, wine, salt and herbs. Cover and cook for 20 minutes, or until chicken is tender, turning pieces once or twice during this time.

There should be just enough liquid left at the end of the cooking time to glaze

the pieces of chicken. Remove lid to concentrate glaze if necessary, or add water if mixture dries out too soon.

Sprinkle with finely chopped parsley before serving with new potatoes and Savoury Beans and Tomatoes (page 78).

MOROCCAN CHICKEN

In Morocco this dish is made with preserved, salted lemons, but as we don't usually have these on hand, we've found fresh lemons are just fine! While the flavour may not be quite the same it's still delicious.

For 4 servings:
1 large onion
3 or 4 cloves garlic
3 Tbsp olive oil
1 Tbsp tomato paste
1 tsp ground cumin
1 tsp paprika
1/2 tsp ground ginger
1/2 tsp salt
juice of 1 lemon
2 Tbsp chopped coriander leaves
4 large bone-in chicken pieces or
    8 drumsticks
1 lemon
15–20 black olives

Chop the onion and garlic finely, using a food processor, if available. Add the next eight ingredients and mix to a thick paste.

Place the chicken in a shallow casserole dish and cover with the paste mixture. Turn the chicken pieces, ensuring they are evenly coated with the mixture. Add the remaining lemon, cut lengthways into eighths, and the olives.

If possible, allow to stand for 1–2 hours (or overnight in the fridge). Bake at 180°C for 1 hour, covered loosely for the first 30 minutes, then uncovered.

Variations:
• For a less lemony flavour use strips of lemon rind instead of lemon wedges.
• Replace lemon wedges with the skin of one preserved salted lemon, if available.

Serve with plain rice or Spicy Rice Pilaf (page 82), which can be baked at the same time, and Spinach Salad (page 86).

SPRING CHICKEN AND VEGETABLE CASSEROLE

This tasty family dinner may be prepared ahead and left to turn itself on in an automatic oven, or assembled just before baking.

For 4 servings:
8 bone-in chicken pieces or 1 jointed
    chicken
1 Tbsp oil
12–20 button mushrooms
4 small new potatoes
8–12 whole small carrots
12–20 button mushrooms
2 tsp chopped fresh tarragon or 1/2 tsp
    dried tarragon
1 cup dry white wine
1 cup chicken stock
cornflour to thicken
1/2 cup finely chopped parsley

Brown the chicken pieces evenly on all sides, in the oil. Transfer to a large casserole and arrange around the chicken the unpeeled potatoes and carrots. Sauté the mushrooms lightly in the pan and add to the casserole.

Sprinkle with tarragon (or use thyme if preferred). Add wine and chicken stock. (Make chicken stock from 1 cup water and 2 level teaspoons instant chicken stock if necessary.)

Cover tightly. Bake at 180°C until potatoes and chicken are cooked (about 1 1/2 hours).

Thicken juices lightly with a paste made of cornflour and water. Just before serving, stir chopped parsley though the liquid.

Serve with Savoury Beans and Tomatoes (page 78).

COUNTRY CAPTAIN CHICKEN

This traditional American recipe makes a very successful party dish.

For 6 servings:
12 bone-in chicken pieces
1/2 cup flour
3–4 Tbsp oil
1 large onion, sliced
1 clove garlic, sliced
1 green pepper, sliced
1 Tbsp brown sugar
2 tsp curry powder
1 tsp salt
1/2 tsp thyme
425g can whole tomatoes
1/4 cup currants

Coat the chicken pieces evenly with flour, then heat the oil in a large frypan and brown over high heat, turning pieces when necessary. Remove from the pan.

Lower the heat and add onion, garlic and green pepper. Cook for 2–3 minutes without browning the vegetables, then replace chicken pieces in the pan, skin-side down. Add sugar, curry powder, salt, thyme and roughly chopped tomatoes and juice. Cover and cook over a low heat for 15 minutes. Turn chicken, add currants, and cook for a further 10–15 minutes, or until juices run clear.

Variation:
For larger numbers arrange browned chicken pieces best side down in a roasting dish. Prepare remaining ingredients in the pan then pour over the chicken. Cover with foil and bake at 180°C for 30 minutes then uncover, turn and cook for 15 minutes longer. (If the mixture is refrigerated before baking, allow 15 minutes longer.)

Serve with curry side dishes (pages 90–91) if desired or with Bread Rolls (page 104) and a Mixed Green Salad (page 86).

Moroccan Chicken ▶

▲ *Festive Chicken in Pastry*

FESTIVE CHICKEN IN PASTRY

Prepare this recipe for a festive dinner for a small group. It looks special, but is not too complicated or time-consuming.

For 3–5 servings:
4 boneless, skinless chicken breasts
2 Tbsp olive oil
1 large onion
1 cup parsley sprigs
1 tsp fresh sage
¼ cup pinenuts
6 spinach leaves
12–15 pieces sun-dried tomatoes or a jar
of Sliced Red Peppers, drained
400g puff pastry
1 egg

Flatten chicken breasts between two plastic bags, using a rolling pin, until each is twice its original width and length.

To make a green stuffing layer, chop the onion, parsley and sage finely and cook in the heated oil until the onion is soft and transparent. Add pinenuts and brown very lightly. Wash and chop the spinach. Cook briefly, until wilted, then drain and stir into the onion mixture.

To make a red layer, use sun-dried tomatoes or Sliced Red Peppers. (Soak chopped tomatoes in a little boiling water for 15 minutes.)

Roll the pastry out until it is 45cm square. Place two of the flattened

chicken breasts side by side on the centre of this, patting into an oval shape. Spread the spinach mixture evenly on top, leaving the edges clear, then arrange the tomatoes or peppers on this. Place remaining chicken on top. Pat into a neat shape. Cut four diagonal lines from the corners of the pastry to the chicken. Fold the pastry over the chicken, trim away excess, but leave enough to fold under the ends. You should finish up with an oval package. Brush with beaten egg.

Bake at 220°C for 45–60 minutes, until golden brown. Cover loosely if the top browns too fast. Allow to stand for 10 minutes before serving.

Serve with seasonal vegetables.

ROASTED CHICKEN LEGS
AND SUMMER VEGETABLES

(See photograph pages 42–43.)
This is an updated, 30-minute version of roast chicken
and vegetables for two people.

For 2 servings:
fresh rosemary sprigs
2 chicken legs
2 peppers, red, green or yellow
1 large red onion
2 small eggplants
2 Tbsp orange juice
2 Tbsp light soya sauce
2 Tbsp olive oil

Place fresh rosemary sprigs over the bottom of a roasting dish (preferably one with a non-stick surface). Place chicken legs on top.

Quarter the peppers and remove the seeds. Peel and quarter the onion, leaving the root end intact. Quarter the eggplants lengthways. Put the prepared vegetables on the rosemary around the chicken pieces.

Mix together the orange juice, soya sauce and oil. Brush the chicken and vegetables with this mixture.

Bake at 220°C for 25–30 minutes, basting the chicken and vegetables once or twice during this time. Test the chicken by piercing with a skewer in the thickest part. The chicken is cooked when the juices run clear, not pink.

Serve hot, or at room temperature, with warmed Bread Rolls (page 104).

ROAST LEMON CHICKEN

We don't know why it looks more exciting to have a large, whole bird than a jointed one, but the fact remains that it does!

For 4–8 servings:
1 medium-to-large chicken
1 lemon
3 cloves garlic
2 or 3 sprigs fresh tarragon, thyme or oreganum (optional)
25g butter, melted
¼ cup white wine
½ tsp salt
freshly ground black pepper

Thaw the chicken if necessary, remove giblets etc. Wash and pat dry inside and out.

Make about eight deep cuts in the lemon, without slicing right through, and flatten two cloves of the garlic. Put the cut lemon, garlic and herbs of your choice inside the cavity of the chicken.

Place chicken breast-side up on a rack, so it will cook evenly, and any fat will drip away as it cooks. Combine the butter, wine, salt and pepper, and the remaining clove of garlic, flattened. Brush the chicken with this mixture.

Bake at 200°C for about 1 hour, basting several times during cooking with the liquid around the chicken. The chicken is cooked when the juice from the thickest part of the thigh is clear, not pink, when pierced with a skewer.

Lift chicken onto a serving plate. Skim the juices and serve the remaining liquid over the sliced meat if you like.

Variation:
Brush chicken with a little olive oil instead of the butter and wine mixture. Cook without further seasoning.

Serve garnished with twists of lemon peel and a Spinach or Mixed Green Salad (page 86) or freshly cooked vegetables.

CHEAT'S 'ROAST' CHICKEN

This prizewinning recipe tastes like roast chicken with stuffing and gravy, but eliminates all the last-minute work of a roast dinner.

For 4–6 servings:
1 chicken
1 cup water
1 Tbsp dark soya sauce
2 cloves garlic, finely chopped
cornflour to thicken
salt and pepper to taste
1 onion, finely chopped
2 Tbsp butter
½ tsp oreganum
½ tsp thyme
1 cup fresh breadcrumbs

Place chicken (whole or jointed) in a pot with the water, soya sauce and garlic. Cover and simmer over a low heat for about an hour, or until flesh is tender. Bone chicken and place meat in a shallow ovenware dish. Strain liquid and thicken with cornflour paste to gravy consistency. Add extra seasonings to taste and pour over chicken.

Cook onion in butter until tender but not browned. Remove from heat and mix well with the crumbled dried herbs and breadcrumbs. Spread topping evenly over cooled sauce and chicken.

Cover and refrigerate until required (overnight if you like). Reheat, uncovered, at 190°C until topping is crisp and sauce and chicken have heated through, about 30–40 minutes.

Variation:
Add chopped sautéed mushrooms to boned chicken and sauce mixture.

Serve with boiled new potatoes, or roast potatoes, green beans or broccoli and carrots.

ROAST STUFFED CHICKEN WITH GRAVY

A stuffed roast chicken is often the centrepiece of a special-occasion family meal.

For 6 servings:
1 size 7–9 chicken (about 1.5kg)
stuffing (see below)
1 Tbsp light soya sauce
1 Tbsp lemon juice
3 Tbsp flour
2 cups stock
2 Tbsp sherry (optional)

Thaw chicken slowly if necessary, remove the wrapping and pat dry, inside and out, removing giblets, neck, etc. (Simmer giblets and any trimmings in 3 cups water with vegetable trimmings, for stock for gravy.) Pull away and discard any fat from around the large cavity.

Just before cooking, pack prepared stuffing into main cavity of the bird. (If there is some left over, pack it into the front cavity and/or wrap it in buttered foil to bake beside the chicken for 30 minutes.) Secure openings with toothpicks or sew with a heavy needle and thread. Place bird breast-side up on baking paper or a piece of non-stick Teflon liner.

Mix light soya sauce and lemon juice and rub over all outer surfaces. Bake at 180–200°C for about 1½ hours surrounded by roast vegetables if you like. (A stuffed bird takes longer to cook than an unstuffed one.) Baste with remaining soya and lemon while bird cooks.

To test to see whether bird is cooked, pierce the inner thigh with a skewer. If juices are clear, not pink, it is cooked.

Transfer bird (and roast vegetables) to serving plate. Drain off fat, leaving pan drippings and about a tablespoon of fat. Stir flour into this and heat until it bubbles and browns. Add about 2 cups of strained stock and/or vegetable cooking liquid, with a dash of sherry. Simmer for at least 5 minutes, then season and strain into a serving jug.

Traditional Herbed Stuffing:
1 onion, finely chopped
1 stalk celery, very finely chopped
1–2 Tbsp butter
1 tsp grated orange or lemon rind (optional)
¼ cup chopped parsley
1 tsp chopped fresh thyme or ½ tsp dried thyme leaves or other herbs
1 egg yolk or white
salt and pepper (optional)
4 slices stale bread, crumbled

Cook onion and celery in a covered pan for 3–5 minutes without browning. Remove from the heat. Add remaining ingredients and mix well.

Variations:
• Replace breadcrumbs with 1½ cups cooked brown or white rice, or cooked rice-shaped pasta.

• Cook ½–1 chopped apple with the onion and celery.
• Replace half the breadcrumbs with chopped cooked mushrooms.
• Add chopped ham, cooked bacon, etc., to Traditional Stuffing.
• Use minced chicken stuffing (see Roast Boned Chicken below).

Dried Apricot with Pinenuts:
1 onion, finely chopped
1 Tbsp butter or oil
¼ cup currants
¼ cup pinenuts
3 thick slices bread, crumbed
¼–½ cup dried apricots, chopped and soaked
1 beaten egg yolk or white (optional)

Cook chopped onion in butter or oil until transparent, add currants and pinenuts and cook until plumped and lightly browned. Stir in crumbed bread, and apricots. For a firmer stuffing, stir egg into mixture.

Roast Stuffed Chicken Legs:
Make a small amount of stuffing. Separate skin from flesh on outer side of a leg, pack stuffing into this, between flesh and skin, secure with a toothpick.

Roast stuffing-side up, at 180°C for 45 minutes or until juices run clear when chicken is pierced deeply.

ROAST BONED CHICKEN

Although it takes 15 minutes, a little patience and a sharp knife to bone a chicken, the resulting bird is very easy to carve and is a great talking point.

For 6–8 servings:
1 size 8–10 chicken
400g minced chicken or breast meat
1 egg
¼ cup cream
2 Tbsp dry sherry
1 tsp salt
½ cup finely chopped fresh herbs
1 onion
2 tsp butter
2 Tbsp tomato paste

Starting by cutting from neck to tail down the centre back, cut around rib cage, then remove all bones from the chicken, leaving the leg and wing bones in place. Lie chicken flat, skin-side down. (Boil all bones and scraps to make stock for gravy.)

In a food processor, purée together the chopped chicken breast or mince, the egg, cream, sherry and salt. Remove half the purée, add the herbs to the processor, and mix thoroughly. Put the herb mixture in spoonfuls on the boned chicken.

Chop the onion, cook until tender in the butter, then add with the tomato paste to the remaining puréed chicken. Put this in spoonfuls between the herbed

mixture. Bring edges of the skin to the centre, and sew or skewer together, closing all openings.

Roast, in a roasting dish lined with baking paper or a non-stick Teflon liner, breast-side up, at 180°C for 1½ hours, basting occasionally with oil, melted butter or pan juices.

To carve:
Cut off the legs and wings, then carve into 1cm slices, starting from the front of the bird.

Variation:
Replace tomato paste with 1 cup of finely chopped, cooked mushrooms.

Serve hot with seasonal vegetables or cold with a salad (pages 84–87).

APPLE AND HERB ROASTED TURKEY

*Cook an impressive turkey breast this way next time you are entertaining friends
or business colleagues. It isn't difficult and it looks great.*

For 6–8 servings:

*1 whole turkey breast on the bone
   (1.75kg)
2 large onions, quartered
2 cups water
2 tsp instant chicken stock
½ cup apple juice concentrate
½ cup dry white wine
large sprigs sage or tarragon
400–500g medium-sized mushrooms
2 apples
1 Tbsp cornflour*

Thaw the turkey, if necessary. Rinse and pat dry inside and out. Remove giblets etc. from neck cavity and put into a large roasting dish with the onions.

Combine water, instant stock, apple juice and wine. Pour over the prepared turkey and onions. Place sprigs of herbs on top and under the turkey.

Bake, uncovered at 160°C for 1½–1¾ hours, or according to the instructions on the turkey pack, basting every 15 minutes.

The turkey is cooked when the inner thigh is pierced with a skewer and the juices that run are clear, not pink. Take care not to overcook or the lean turkey meat will dry out.

Lift turkey from the pan onto a large serving dish and keep warm for at least 15 minutes before carving. Remove the onions and arrange around the turkey.

Bring the remaining liquid to the boil in the roasting dish, over a fairly high heat on the cook-top until reduced to about a cup. Cook the mushrooms in this liquid for 2 minutes per side, arrange around the turkey. Cut the cored but unpeeled apples into 1cm slices and cook in the liquid until barely tender, about 5 minutes. Remove from the pan and arrange attractively.

Skim the remaining liquid and thicken with 1 tablespoon of cornflour mixed with a little water.

Serve thickened liquid separately.

59

Vegetarian Mains

This chapter offers an interesting and varied selection of vegetarian main dishes for the semi-vegetarian who wants to eat several main meals each week, which do not include chicken or fish.

Choose from pasta-based dishes, egg, cheese and vegetable mixtures, recipes based on grains, and those using dried peas, beans and lentils. (Look in the soup and starters sections for more recipes, too.)

A wide variety of seasonings have been used in the recipes. At one end of the scale are gently flavoured family favourites, suitable for young families, and at the other, interesting spicy sauces to give new life to bland foods.

The selection here, although varied, is far from comprehensive. If you want more vegetarian recipes, we suggest you use our very popular earlier book, Meals Without Meat, which contains many more recipes, none of which are in this chapter.

It is always important to remember nutrition guidelines. If you feel you do not eat as many vegetables or grains as you should, choose recipes with these ingredients from this section. And, again, with these guidelines in mind, if you cook the egg-based meals here, do not serve eggs for breakfast or lunch.

◀ **Curried Chickpeas (page 65)**

▲ *Fresh Ravioli Sauce*

FRESH RAVIOLI SAUCE

Fresh ravioli cooks in just a few minutes. This summery sauce is almost as fast! It's just the thing for a really quick meal for a warm evening!

For 3–4 servings:
1 large red pepper
2 Tbsp butter
2 cloves garlic, chopped
425g can Italian Seasoned Tomatoes
1 tsp sugar
2 tsp cornflour
¼ cup water or white wine
2–3 Tbsp chopped fresh herbs
250–300g fresh ravioli (any filling)
parmesan or grated cheddar cheese
        (optional)

Cut the red pepper into small cubes and cook gently in the butter with the garlic, without browning.

Tip the can of tomatoes into this, then simmer uncovered for 2–3 minutes. Mix the sugar and cornflour to a paste with the water or wine. Stir into simmering mixture, add the fresh herbs and season to taste.

Cook your favourite fresh ravioli in plenty of boiling salted water, following the instructions on the packet, until just cooked.

Spoon sauce over the freshly cooked, lightly buttered ravioli, or add the drained, cooked ravioli to the sauce and turn gently to mix.

Serve plain, or topped with grated parmesan or cheddar cheese.

62

MUSHROOM STROGANOFF

Mushrooms in a rich sauce make a quick meal with an interesting texture.

For 4–5 servings:
750g mushrooms (preferably medium-
    sized partly open)
1–2 Tbsp butter or olive oil
2 cloves garlic, chopped
1 Tbsp flour
1 cup chicken stock
1 Tbsp tomato paste
2 Tbsp sherry
¼–½ cup sour cream
1 bunch spring onions, chopped
about 400g fresh or dried spaghetti or
    other (green if you like) pasta
1 Tbsp butter, oil or pesto

Choose medium-sized partly open mushrooms for maximum flavour and colour. Cut in quarters and cook in butter or oil with chopped garlic over high heat, until lightly browned. Stir in the flour and cook for about 3 minutes. Add the chicken stock, tomato paste and sherry and simmer for 5 minutes. Stir in sour cream to taste, with half the spring onions.

Cook the pasta in plenty of boiling, lightly salted water until just tender. Drain and toss in a little butter, oil or pesto.

Serve sauce on the pasta and sprinkle with remaining spring onions. Good with a crisp green salad.

SIMPLE PASTA SAUCE

This simple and delicious pasta sauce can easily be dressed up to make the basis of an elegant and substantial meal.

For 2–3 servings:
250–300g fresh or dried pasta (any
    shape)
2–3 Tbsp butter
¼ cup cream
¼ cup grated parmesan cheese
freshly ground black pepper
extra parmesan cheese to serve

Cook the pasta according to the instructions on the packet, in plenty of boiling, lightly salted water.

Drain, then add the butter and toss through the pasta. Pour on the cream, sprinkle over the parmesan, then mix lightly. Add pepper to taste. Allow to stand for a minute or so, stir again, then serve, with extra parmesan.

To dress up:

Simply toss in your choice of one or two of the following: pesto, chopped fresh herbs, slivers of smoked salmon, lightly cooked asparagus, zucchini, sugar peas, broccoli florets, strips of sun-dried tomato, halved cherry tomatoes or a little crumbled blue cheese.

Served with salad (pages 84–87), this makes an easy meal in about 10 minutes!

ARTICHOKE HEART AND TOMATO PASTA

The artichoke hearts and sun-dried tomatoes used in this pasta dish are fairly expensive, but they make a delicious occasional treat.

For 4 servings:
1 large onion
2 Tbsp oil
2 cloves garlic, finely chopped
1 green pepper
425g can whole tomatoes
½ tsp each chilli powder and salt
1 tsp balsamic vinegar (optional)
1 Tbsp each pesto and capers
4 canned or bottled artichoke hearts
¼ cup sun-dried tomatoes
400g fresh pasta
butter
parmesan cheese

Quarter then peel the onion, and cut into 5mm slices.

Heat the oil in a large frypan, add the onion and garlic and cook until the onion has softened but not browned. Add the quartered and sliced green pepper and cook for a few minutes longer.

Add the roughly chopped tomatoes and their juice and cook for about 5 minutes, stirring occasionally, until the sauce has thickened. Stir in the chilli powder, salt, vinegar, pesto and capers.

Turn off the heat, but leave the pan on the element. Quarter the artichoke hearts and chop the sun-dried tomatoes into 1cm strips. Stir the artichoke and tomato pieces gently through the sauce mixture.

Meanwhile, cook the pasta according to packet instructions, until barely tender in plenty of boiling salted water. Drain well, and toss with a little butter.

Serve in large bowl or individual plates, with sauce spooned over the pasta. Sprinkle with parmesan cheese.

▲ *Super Special Macaroni Cheese*

SUPER SPECIAL MACARONI CHEESE

*Turn macaroni cheese into something special! The sauce that coats the macaroni
is very carefully seasoned, and tastes 'extra cheesy'!*

For 4–6 servings:

300g macaroni, or other pasta
50g butter
1 tsp curry powder
¼ cup flour
3 cups milk
1 Tbsp Dijon mustard
1 tsp salt
¼ tsp freshly ground pepper
1 tsp Worcestershire sauce
½ tsp Tabasco sauce
½ tsp grated nutmeg
2 cups grated tasty cheese

Topping:

1–2 Tbsp butter
1 cup fresh breadcrumbs
½ cup grated tasty cheese

Cook the macaroni in a large pot of
boiling, lightly salted water. Rinse with
cold water and leave to drain in a sieve.

Melt the butter in a pot, add the curry
powder then the flour and heat until it
bubbles. Add the milk a cup at a time,
bringing to the boil and stirring
constantly between additions. Stir in the
remaining ingredients and stir to
combine, without reheating. Carefully
stir the macaroni and sauce together,
and turn into a well-buttered or sprayed
12-cup-capacity ovenware dish.

For the topping, melt butter and remove
from heat. Stir in breadcrumbs and
cheese, and sprinkle over the surface of
the macaroni cheese.

Bake at 180°C for 30 minutes or until
the sauce bubbles and the top browns.

*This is particularly good served with
Spinach Salad (page 86).*

64

VEGETABLE LASAGNE

Mixtures of savoury foods layered between lasagne noodles have become so popular in recent years that they are now considered part of our basic cuisine.

For 6 servings:
First layer:
1 onion, finely chopped
1 clove garlic, finely chopped
1 Tbsp olive oil
about 300g mushrooms, sliced
1 tsp fresh thyme, finely chopped
1 cup vegetable stock
1 Tbsp cornflour
¼ cup water
salt and pepper to taste

Second layer:
300g broccoli or spinach, chopped
1 cup (250g) cottage cheese
2 eggs
1 cup grated tasty cheese
salt and pepper

250g fresh lasagne sheets (spinach or plain)
425g can Italian Seasoned Tomatoes
½ cup grated tasty cheese

First layer:
Cook the onion and garlic in the oil until soft but not browned. Add the mushrooms and thyme, and cook for 5 minutes more. Add the vegetable stock, then thicken with the cornflour, mixed with ¼ cup water. Season to taste.

Second layer:
Cook the broccoli or spinach until barely tender. Drain. Mix together the cottage cheese, eggs, grated cheese, and salt and pepper to taste. Stir in the drained broccoli or spinach.

To assemble:
Butter or spray a casserole dish about 20 x 30cm. Cover with a layer of lasagne sheets. Spread with the mushroom mixture then top with a second layer of lasagne sheets. Spoon the cottage cheese mixture over this, and cover with more lasagne. Pour the tomato mixture evenly over the top, covering it completely. Sprinkle with the grated cheese.

Cover and bake at 180°C for about 40–45 minutes. Remove cover and bake for about 15 minutes longer, until the top is lightly browned.

Serve with one of our suggested salads (pages 84–87).

LAYERED MACARONI BAKE

This basic, easy recipe is very popular with children and offers a good way to use up leftovers.

For 4 servings:
300g large macaroni shapes
1 Tbsp butter
1 Tbsp flour
425g can Italian Tomatoes
cooked mushrooms, corn or other vegetables (optional)
1 cup grated cheese
2 eggs
1 cup milk

Cook the macaroni in plenty of lightly salted boiling water until tender, then drain, and stir through the butter, flour and tomatoes. Stir in additional vegetables if you like, and spread in a 20–24cm ovenware dish, smoothing the top so it is reasonably compacted and level.

Sprinkle evenly with grated cheese. Beat the eggs and milk to blend, then pour over the pasta and cheese mixture.

Bake uncovered at 180°C for 30–40 minutes or until the cheesy topping is firm in the centre. Allow to stand for 5–10 minutes before serving.

Serve with broccoli, beans, a green salad, or coleslaw.

CURRIED CHICKPEAS

(See photograph pages 60–61.)
This dish is delicious served on its own or as part of an Indian-style meal.

For 6 servings:
4 cups cooked chickpeas
1 large onion, chopped
2 cloves garlic, chopped
1 Tbsp butter
1 tsp grated fresh ginger
1 tsp turmeric
1 tsp ground cumin
½ tsp cinnamon
¼ tsp ground cloves
¼–½ tsp chilli powder
425g can whole tomatoes
1 tsp salt
sugar (optional)

Soak 1½ cups of dried chickpeas in water overnight then boil in unsalted water for about 2 hours or until tender, or use about 4 cups of canned chickpeas, drained.

In a large pot cook the onion and garlic in the butter until transparent but not browned, then stir in the seasonings (using the smaller amount of chilli powder for a fairly mild flavour) and cook for a few minutes longer. Add the tomatoes, then the drained chickpeas, and cook gently for about 15 minutes. Break up slightly with a potato masher to thicken the mixture, if you like. Add salt and a little sugar to taste if you have started with dried chickpeas.

Serve in bowls with rice and curry accompaniments (pages 90–91) or a green salad.

▲ *Crunchy Curried Cauliflower*

CRUNCHY CURRIED CAULIFLOWER

The seasonings used in this recipe are interesting, but not too hot. You can change the hotness by using more or less chilli powder if you like.

For about 6 servings:

2 Tbsp each sesame and cumin seeds
2 cloves garlic, finely chopped
1½ tsp grated fresh ginger
2 Tbsp roasted peanuts, finely chopped
½ tsp turmeric
¼ tsp chilli powder
½ tsp ground cloves
1 tsp salt
2–3 Tbsp oil
2 medium-sized onions, chopped
1 large cauliflower, cut into walnut-
*   sized florets*
juice of ½ lemon

Toast the sesame seeds, then the cumin seeds in a frypan, without any added oil. Grind the seeds, separately or mixed, add the garlic, ginger, peanuts, turmeric, chilli powder, ground cloves and salt, and put aside.

Heat the oil and cook the onions until transparent and lightly coloured. Stir the spice mixture through the onion, then add the cauliflower florets. Add the lemon juice and about ¼ cup of water,

cover, and cook over a moderate heat, stirring and tossing the cauliflower occasionally, until it is tender-crisp. Taste and add extra salt if necessary.

Serve with cooked rice, tomato or cucumber salad and/or other curry accompaniments (pages 90–91).

66

CURRIED POTATOES

This potato curry is an easy microwave recipe. Quarter the recipe, reducing all the microwaving times to about a third, and you have a good quick meal for one.

For 4 servings:
1 onion, chopped
8 small potatoes (800–900g)
425ml can coconut cream
2 tsp curry powder
½–1 tsp salt
½ tsp sugar
1–2 cups frozen peas
about 300g cauliflower florets (optional)
1–2 cups chopped cabbage (optional)

Put the onion and the unpeeled, halved or quartered potatoes into a microwave dish with the coconut cream and seasonings, adding the smaller amount of salt.

Stir to mix, cover, and microwave on High (100% power) for 12 minutes, repositioning potatoes once or twice, until potatoes are barely tender.

Add the frozen peas, and microwave for about 4 minutes, or add the peas, cauliflower and cabbage, stir to coat vegetables, then microwave for 6–8 minutes, stirring at least once during the cooking time. Check that the cauliflower and cabbage are cooked to the tender-crisp stage, and taste the sauce, adjusting the seasonings if necessary.

Serve immediately, or allow to stand, then reheat when required. Pile in bowls, and serve with Bread Rolls (page 104).

PANEER CHEESE

This is an Indian style of cheese. It tastes rather like cottage cheese, but its texture is quite firm. Rather like tofu, alone it is fairly bland, but is a good protein 'base'.

For 2–3 servings:
2 litres milk
50–60ml lemon juice

Pour the milk into a large pot, and heat slowly, stirring occasionally, until boiling.

Remove the pot from the heat and gradually add the lemon juice, while stirring continuously. The milk should separate, producing thick, whitish curd and clear whey. Leave to cool for a few minutes, stirring every now and then.

Line a large sieve or colander with cheesecloth or a teatowel, and then strain the milk mixture, discarding the whey. Stand the sieve over a pot or bowl, and then place a small plate on top of the curds, and a weight on top of this (the milk container full of water works well). Allow to stand for several hours or, better still, overnight.

You should be left with around 300g of paneer cheese, which will keep quite well in the refrigerator for several days, until required.

PANEER IN SPICY TOMATO CURRY

Paneer alone is fairly bland, and is best served in some sort of well-flavoured sauce.

For 2–3 large servings:
2 large onions
2 or 3 cloves garlic
3 Tbsp oil
2.5cm cinnamon stick
2 bay leaves
10 black peppercorns
4 whole cloves
3 cardamom pods
1 tsp ground cumin
½ tsp each coriander, chilli powder, fenugreek seeds, turmeric, and mustard seeds
425g can whole tomatoes
½ tsp salt
1 tsp sugar
1 tsp garam masala
300–400g paneer cheese, cubed (recipe above)

Chop the onions and garlic in a food processor. Heat the oil in a large frypan over a moderate heat then add the onion and garlic. Cook for about 10 minutes, stirring frequently to prevent burning. When the mixture is very soft, and beginning to brown, add all the spices (except the garam masala) and stir over the heat for 3 minutes.

Stir in the tomatoes, salt, sugar and garam masala. Take off the heat, remove the bay leaves and cinnamon stick. Process the mixture until smooth. Put back in the pan, add the cubed paneer and heat through.

Variation:
Replace paneer cheese with the same amount of firm tofu.

Serve on rice with your favourite curry accompaniments (pages 90–91).

FESTIVE QUICHE

Make this colourful quiche when you want a quick meal.

For 6 servings:
200g flaky pastry
400g can whole tomatoes
3 cups broccoli florets
3 eggs
$\frac{1}{2}$ cup cream
$\frac{1}{4}$ cup milk
$\frac{1}{4}$ cup grated parmesan cheese
$\frac{1}{2}$ tsp salt

Roll pastry out thinly and use it to line a 20cm flan tin with a removable base and 5cm sides. Run a rolling pin over the top to cut off the pastry edges.

Chop tomatoes roughly and drain well. Cook the broccoli in a little water, for about 2 minutes or until barely tender, then drain well.

Mix together the eggs, cream, milk, parmesan cheese and salt, with a fork until well combined.

Fill the uncooked pastry base with the cooled broccoli, pour the egg mixture over it, and arrange the tomato pieces on top.

Bake at 220°C for 15 minutes, until the pastry edge has browned, then lower the oven temperature to 175°C and cook for about 10 minutes longer, or until the mixture has set in the centre.

As soon as the quiche is removed from the oven, remove the sides of the flan tin so the pastry will remain crisp.

Serve warm or reheated with a salad (pages 84–87) and Bread Rolls (page 104).

LAYERED ZUCCHINI AND MUSHROOM CASSEROLE

This dish can stand alone as the main part of a meal, but it is also a popular addition to a buffet meal.

For 4 servings:
1–2 Tbsp oil or butter
1 onion, chopped
2 cloves garlic, finely chopped
200g mushrooms, sliced
500g zucchini, finely sliced or coarsely grated
1 cup grated cheese
2 eggs
$\frac{1}{2}$ cup (125g) sour cream
1 Tbsp pesto or 2 Tbsp chopped fresh basil
$\frac{1}{2}$ tsp salt
$\frac{1}{4}$ cup milk
paprika and grated parmesan cheese

Heat the oil or butter in a frypan and cook the onion and garlic until the onion is soft and translucent. Add the mushrooms, and cook until wilted.

Mix the zucchini with the grated cheese. Spread half of this mixture over the bottom of a well-buttered or sprayed 18 x 25cm baking dish. Cover with the onion and mushroom mixture, then the other half of the zucchini and cheese.

Beat together the eggs, sour cream, pesto and salt. This should make an easily pourable mixture, but if it is very thick, add the milk. Pour this mixture over the layered zucchini and mushrooms, then top with a sprinkling of paprika and grated parmesan cheese.

Bake uncovered, at 175°C for 30–40 minutes, until top is brown and centre is firm.

Serve with buttered new potatoes or rice, and a salad (pages 84–87).

POTATOES TO DIE FOR!

This potato recipe is delicious if rather sinful, since it contains rather a lot of sour cream. Serve it as an occasional treat.

For 4 main servings:
1$\frac{1}{2}$ kg potatoes (Desiree for preference)
3 large cloves garlic
$\frac{1}{4}$ cup flour
$\frac{1}{2}$ tsp salt
2 cups sour cream
$\frac{1}{2}$ cup milk
200g gruyere cheese, grated

Scrub the potatoes, cut in 5mm slices, and drop into a large container of cold water. Drain and transfer to a microwave dish or oven bag, cover bowl or tie bag loosely, and microwave until the potatoes are tender, 12–15 minutes on High (100% power).

Make the sauce while the potatoes cook. Using a food processor if available, finely chop the garlic, then add the flour, salt, sour cream and milk. Process until smooth.

Butter or spray a large shallow oval or rectangular baking dish, about 23 x 30cm. Overlap half the potatoes in it, drizzle almost half the sauce mixture over them, then sprinkle over almost half of the cheese. Repeat with the remaining potatoes and cream sauce, and then sprinkle the rest of the cheese evenly over the top.

Bake uncovered at 180°C for about 30 minutes, until the potatoes have heated through and the topping is golden brown. Allow to stand in a warm place for 5–10 minutes before serving.

Variation:
Top with 200–300g of hot smoked salmon, broken into flakes, as soon as you remove from the oven.

Serve with a Mixed Green Salad or a Spinach Salad (page 86).

Quick Corn Square ▲

QUICK CORN SQUARE

Just the thing when you want to make a quick, easy, tasty meal for the family or unexpected guests!

For 6–8 servings:
4 large eggs
440g can cream-style corn
½ cup sour cream
2 cups grated tasty cheese
½ cup self-raising flour
½ tsp garlic salt
2 spring onions, finely chopped
400g can whole tomatoes, drained
(optional)

Put the eggs, corn and sour cream in a large bowl. Stir with a fork until well mixed. Sprinkle over this the cheese, flour and garlic salt, and half the chopped spring onions, and stir just enough to mix. Drain then chop the tomatoes (if used) and stir them gently through the mixture. Pour into a lightly buttered or sprayed 20cm square baking pan.

Sprinkle with the remaining spring onions and bake uncovered at 180°C for 30 minutes or until set in the centre and lightly browned on top.

Serve hot, warm, or reheated with an interesting mixed salad or coleslaw.

69

▲ *Green Rice with Tomatoes & Savoury Beans and Tomatoes (page 78)*

GREEN RICE WITH TOMATOES

Good warm or reheated, served with salads this makes an interesting family meal or addition to a summer buffet.

For 6–8 servings:

1½ cups basmati rice
3 cups boiling water
500g spinach
2 cups grated tasty cheese
1 tsp grated nutmeg
4 eggs
1 cup milk
2 cloves garlic, finely chopped
2 Tbsp chopped fresh herbs or 1 Tbsp pesto
425g can Mexican Tomatoes
1 cup grated tasty cheese

Cook the rice in a pot of lightly salted boiling water on the stove or for about 12 minutes on High (100% power) in the microwave oven. Allow to stand for 5 minutes if microwaved, then drain if necessary.

In another container, cook the spinach until barely tender, then drain well, squeezing out all the water. Chop finely and add to the cooked rice with the first measure of cheese, nutmeg, eggs, milk, garlic and herbs or pesto.

Bake uncovered, at 200°C in a roasting dish, for about 15 minutes or until it

feels firm. Spread tomatoes evenly over the hot rice, sprinkle with the second measure of grated cheese, and bake for 10 minutes longer, until the cheese melts.

Variation:

Replace white rice with the same amount of brown rice. Cook longer, until completely tender, before mixing with the other ingredients.

Serve hot, warm, or reheated, cut into squares with a crisp leafy salad.

MUSHROOM RISOTTO

Risottos do require some attention while they cook, but this only takes about 20 minutes.
The finished result should be creamy, but the rice grains should remain intact.

For 3 servings:
2–3 Tbsp oil
2 medium-sized onions, chopped
2 cloves garlic, chopped
250g mushrooms
1 cup arborio (or short-grain) rice
½ cup white wine
2–3 cups mushroom, vegetable or
*   chicken stock, or 3 tsp instant stock*
*   powder and 3 cups water*
1 cup frozen peas
¼ cup cream (optional)
¼–½ cup grated parmesan cheese

Heat the oil in a large pot or frypan and cook the onion and garlic until soft, then add the mushrooms and cook until wilted, over a fairly high heat. Stir in the rice and continue to cook, stirring frequently until the rice has turned milky white.

Add the wine and stir until it has all been absorbed by the rice. Pour in the first cup of stock and stir frequently until this too has been absorbed (around 5 minutes).

Add another ½ cup of stock and leave to simmer, stirring occasionally and adding more stock ¼–½ cup at a time

as required, for 10–15 minutes. When the rice is cooked (still firm to bite but with no grainy centre), add the peas and the cream.

Cook over a low heat until the peas are tender, then remove from the heat and stir in the grated parmesan.

Serve immediately, with a tomato salad or Mixed Green Salad (page 86).

BROWN RICE SALAD

This salad has a lovely flavour. Served cold or warm it makes an excellent
addition to a buffet and makes an interesting vegetarian meal.

For 6 servings:
1 cup uncooked brown rice
1¾ cups water
¼ cup light soya sauce
½ medium-sized onion, finely chopped
3 spring onions, finely chopped
1 red pepper, chopped into tiny cubes
½ cup sultanas
½ cup roasted peanuts, coarsely chopped
½ cup each of roasted sunflower,
*   pumpkin, and sesame seeds*

Place rice and unsalted water in a tightly covered pot and simmer for 45 minutes, until the rice is tender and the water has all been absorbed.

Add the soya sauce and finely chopped onion to the hot, cooked rice, mix well, then leave for at least 2 hours or overnight if you have the time.

After this standing time, add the remaining ingredients. Toss the dressing through the salad.

For best flavour, serve straight away, or a short time after adding the dressing.

Dressing:
¼ cup olive or other oil
2 Tbsp lemon juice
1 tsp grated lemon rind
1 clove garlic, crushed
1 tsp grated fresh root ginger
1 tsp honey or sugar

Combine all ingredients and process until smooth using a food processor, or shake well in a screw-topped jar.

Use with Pumpkin Bake (below) or with Spinach Salad (page 86).

PUMPKIN BAKE

Here is an easy, good and substantial recipe that I invented on the spur of the
moment, one day when I wanted to serve pumpkin as one of the main parts of a meal.

For 6 servings:
800g pumpkin, cooked
2 eggs
½ cup cream
½ cup milk
½ tsp ground cardamom (or cinnamon)
½ tsp salt
freshly ground black pepper to taste
2 cups grated tasty cheese

Weigh the pumpkin before cooking, after removing seeds etc. Using a tablespoon, scoop pieces of pumpkin into a lightly sprayed or buttered casserole dish that is large enough to hold it in one layer. Do not smooth the surface completely.

Beat the eggs, cream and milk together with a fork. Add the cardamom, salt and pepper. Pour this evenly over the pumpkin and top with grated cheese.

Bake at 200°C for 20–25 minutes, or until the custard is set, the mixture has puffed up, and the top is brown.

Serve as soon as possible, since it deflates on standing. This is good served with a cooked green vegetable or with Brown Rice Salad (above).

POLENTA AND VEGETABLE CASSEROLE

This recipe sounds more fiddly than it really is. You can eat it less than an hour after you start to make it.

For 4 servings:
2 cups water
1 tsp salt
1 cup coarse yellow cornmeal
½ cup grated cheese
1 large onion, sliced
3 cloves garlic, finely chopped
1 Tbsp oil
1 green or red pepper, chopped
2–2½ cups diced or sliced vegetables
    (e.g. carrots, zucchini, mushrooms)
425g can whole tomatoes
1 Tbsp pesto or 2 Tbsp chopped fresh
    basil
½ tsp marjoram
¼ tsp thyme
salt and pepper to taste
1 cup grated cheese

To make the polenta, bring the water and salt to the boil in a large pot. Slowly sprinkle in the cornmeal, stirring continuously. (It should form a very thick paste as you keep on stirring.) Cook for 3–5 minutes. Remove from the heat and stir in the first measure of grated cheese, then spread over the bottom of a well-buttered or sprayed 22cm square casserole dish or cake tin. Allow to stand while preparing the topping.

Cook the onion and garlic in the oil until soft. Add the pepper and the slower-cooking vegetables and continue to cook for several minutes, stirring occasionally. Add the remaining vegetables, the crushed canned tomatoes and juice, and the seasonings. Simmer until the vegetables are barely tender, then spread over the prepared polenta.

Cover with the second measure of grated cheese and bake at 175°C for about 30 minutes.

Serve alone or with a salad (pages 84–87) and Bread Rolls (page 104) as a substantial meal.

VEGETABLE COUSCOUS

This recipe will fill your kitchen with its fragrant aroma as it simmers. It is really substantial enough to form the basis of a meal.

For 4–6 servings:
1 cup quick-cooking couscous
2 medium-sized onions, sliced
2 or 3 cloves garlic, chopped
2 Tbsp oil
1 tsp each coriander, cumin and
    turmeric
½ tsp each salt and chilli powder
¼ tsp each ground cloves and allspice
425g can whole tomatoes
1 cup cooked or canned chickpeas
2 or 3 medium-sized potatoes
2 carrots
2 cups vegetables (diced kumara,
    zucchini, peas, etc.)
butter

Measure the couscous into a large shallow bowl, cover with about a cup of boiling water and leave to soak.

Cook the onions and garlic in the oil until the onion is soft and transparent. Add the spices and salt and cook for 1–2 minutes longer, stirring continuously.

Chop the tomatoes and add with the juice. Stir in the chickpeas, and the potatoes and carrots cut into 1cm cubes. Cover the pot or pan and simmer for 15–20 minutes, adding the remaining vegetables at intervals (the slower-cooking ones first), so that all are cooked at the same time.

Drain any excess water from the couscous, and toss with a little butter. Spread the couscous over a large plate and top with the cooked vegetable mixture.

Serve alone or with a selection of your favourite curry accompaniments (pages 90–91).

BARLEY LOAF

If you are used to seeing pearl barley only in soup, this recipe may seem a little unusual, but the barley gives this loaf a wonderful texture.

For 4 large servings:
1 cup pearl barley
3 cups boiling water
2 Tbsp oil
2 medium-sized onions, sliced
3 cloves garlic, finely chopped
100g mushrooms, sliced
1 tsp each basil and oreganum
½ tsp each thyme and salt
1 tsp sesame oil
1 Tbsp light soya sauce
3 eggs, lightly beaten
1 cup cooked spinach
1 cup grated cheese

Place the barley in a large pot or microwave bowl, cover with the boiling water. Cook in the microwave, on Medium (50% power), or simmer gently on the stove, for about 30 minutes, until the grains are swollen and tender. Drain off any excess water and allow to stand.

Heat the oil in a large frypan. Cook the onions and garlic until the onions are soft, then add the mushrooms and cook until soft.

Combine the onion mixture with the cooked barley and all the remaining ingredients, except for about half of the grated cheese. Mix thoroughly, then transfer the mixture into a well-buttered or sprayed 20 x 25cm casserole dish. Sprinkle with the remaining cheese (and a little paprika if desired).

Bake at 180°C for about 45 minutes, covering loosely for the first 30 minutes. The loaf is cooked when the top has browned and the centre is firm when pressed.

Serve with baked potatoes or crusty bread and some colourful stir-fried vegetables or a crisp salad.

CAROL'S VEGETABLE STRUDEL

*This recipe was given to us by a friend. She served it to her grown-up sons who
'didn't like vegetables'. They loved it so much they asked for more!*

For 6 servings:

1 carrot, thinly sliced
125g green beans, sliced
150g broccoli florets
30g butter
1 small leek, finely sliced
4 medium-sized mushrooms, sliced
1 small stick celery, sliced
100g bean sprouts (optional)
9 sheets filo pastry
oil or melted butter for brushing
1 cup (100g) grated tasty cheese
2 slices toast bread, crumbled
½ tsp salt
2 Tbsp finely chopped fresh basil or
*   1 Tbsp pesto*

Blanch the carrot, beans and broccoli separately.

Heat the butter in a small frypan and cook the leek until soft, add the mushroom and celery and cook for a further 2 minutes, then add bean sprouts (if used) and the previously blanched vegetables. Toss well and allow to cool.

Take three sheets of filo pastry, lie them side by side, long sides together with the edges slightly overlapping. Brush each sheet lightly with oil or butter. Cover with three more sheets, oil or butter them the same way, then top with the remaining three sheets. You will end up with a large rectangle, three layers thick.

Place the prepared filling over the first third of the rectangle. Mix together the cheese, breadcrumbs, salt and the basil or pesto and sprinkle this over the vegetables. Roll up loosely. Cover the ends of the roll with tinfoil, so the filling will not fall out during cooking.

Place on an oven tray and bake at 190°C for 30–35 minutes, until golden brown.

Serve immediately, with chicken or fish, or as a vegetarian meal with a leafy green salad.

73

▲ *Mushroom and Avocado Melt*

MUSHROOM AND AVOCADO MELT

Melts make quick, spectacular and substantial meals. Always make them just before they are to be eaten. Experiment, putting different toppings on the toasted bread base, beneath the melted cheese.

For 4 servings:
6 large flat mushrooms
Parmesan Dressing
1 flat (foccacia-type) round bread,*
    about 25cm across
2 avocados
1 large red pepper
grated or sliced cheese

* See recipe page 104.

Lightly brush the stem side of the mushrooms with Parmesan Dressing (page 89). Grill until the cheese bubbles, 2–3 minutes. Turn and brush mushroom tops, then grill again.

Cut the loaf of flat bread through its middle, as you would cut a hamburger bun. Brush the cut surfaces with more of the dressing and grill until golden brown and crisp.

Slice the cooked mushrooms and pile on the toasted bread with slices of avocado and strips of red pepper. Top with grated or sliced cheese, using quantities to suit yourself.

Grill until the cheese melts, then cut in wedges.

Variations:
Try artichoke hearts, smoked chicken, smoked salmon, anchovies, tuna, olives, roasted peppers, grilled eggplant slices, tomatoes, pesto, tapenade and different cheeses on melts.

Serve at once. As this is a casual meal to be eaten in the fingers, follow it with raw fruit, to be eaten in the same way.

ZUCCHINI AND RED ONION FRITTERS

These popular little fritters are made with high-protein pea flour. They are particularly popular as finger food for an informal meal.

Makes 12–14 fritters:
1 egg, beaten
1 cup pea flour
¾ cup water
2 tsp garam masala
2 tsp ground cumin
2 tsp coriander
300g (1½ cups) shredded zucchini
1 large red onion
oil

Beat together the egg, pea flour, water and spices to form a smooth batter. Allow to stand for 15 minutes (the mixture will thicken on standing).

Shred unpeeled zucchini in a food processor, using a blade that cuts long matchstick strips if possible. (For longer, neater strips, cut the zucchini into pieces as long as the feed tube is wide, and press them firmly with the 'pusher' as they are shredded.) Cut the onions into rings about the same thickness as the zucchini. Stir the zucchini and onion into the batter.

Heat oil about 5mm deep in a frypan. Drop tablespoons of the mixture into the hot oil and cook for 2–3 minutes, then turn and cook for a further 1–2 minutes. If patties are not golden brown in this time, adjust the heat until they cook nicely. Lift from the pan onto paper towels. Cook the remaining fritters in batches.

Serve immediately while crisp, as finger food with Spicy Yoghurt Sauce (page 91) for dipping, or with Bread Rolls (page 104) and a salad, and with the same sauce spooned over the fritters.

BEANBURGERS

For this recipe you can open a can of kidney beans, or start from scratch, soaking then precooking dried beans.

For 4 servings:
about 2 cups (400g) cooked kidney
    beans
1 large onion, finely chopped
1 Tbsp butter or oil
1 tsp oreganum
1 tsp ground cumin
1 tsp curry powder
1 tsp salt
1 tsp sugar
1 egg
about ¼ cup dried breadcrumbs

Drain the cooked beans thoroughly.

In a frypan cook the onion in the butter or oil over a medium heat until evenly browned and tender, about 15 minutes.

Stir in all the seasonings and remove from the heat. Mash the drained beans with a fork and add to the seasoned onion. Mix in the egg with a fork, then add enough dried breadcrumbs to make a mixture just firm enough to form into eight soft patties. If necessary, add more breadcrumbs.

Coat the patties with more crumbs then cook in a film of oil in a large pan for about 10 minutes per side.

Serve with your favourite relish or sliced peppers, lettuce, etc., in toasted hamburger buns.

SPICED NUT CUTLETS

Here it is — our version of the original 'nut cutlet'. If handled carefully, these can be barbecued quite successfully.

For 8 burgers:
½ cup unblanched peanuts
½ cup cashew nuts (or almonds)
½ cup pinenuts
½ cup sunflower seeds
2 slices bread
1 medium-sized onion
1 carrot
2 eggs
2 tsp dark soya sauce
½ tsp garlic salt
½ tsp ground cumin
½ tsp chilli powder (optional)
1 Tbsp chopped coriander leaves
    (optional)
black pepper
1–2 Tbsp oil

Place the nuts and sunflower seeds in a food processor and chop until the mixture resembles coarse breadcrumbs.

Remove the nuts, and process the bread into crumbs, add these to the chopped nuts. Peel and quarter the onion and roughly chop the carrot. Process these until finely chopped.

Add the eggs and the seasonings and process briefly, then combine with the chopped nuts and breadcrumbs. Mix thoroughly, then divide the mixture into eight portions and shape into patties.

Heat the oil in large frypan and cook for about 5 minutes a side, until firm when pressed in the middle, and golden brown.

To barbecue:
Brush patties with oil, cook as above on a hot plate, or place in a folding wire rack (now available in most barbecue shops) and cook until browned and firm.

Serve with sweet chilli sauce or Peanut Sauce (page 115) in toasted buns with all the trimmings!

Vegetables and Side Dishes

An interesting cooked vegetable, salad, or grainy dish served alongside the main dish can make all the difference to the colour, texture and flavour balance of your meal.

In this chapter we offer you many ideas — some that are very quick and easy, and others which are a bit more complicated, suitable for times when you are cooking for friends.

From the point of view of good nutrition, it is often better for us to eat a smaller portion of the main dish, and a larger amount of the foods in this chapter. This idea is likely to be kinder to your budget, too, unless you choose vegetables that are out of season. Vegetables are inevitably plumper, brighter and have maximum flavour when they are in season, too, so it always makes sense to make the most of them at this time.

Bread, rice, pasta and beans are great fillers for hungry adolescents and are also inexpensive. Use them often!

◀ **Roasted Pepper Salad and Pasta Salad (page 81)**

CAULIFLOWER IN CURRIED TOMATO SAUCE

This sauce turns cauliflower into something really special!

For 4–6 servings:
500g prepared cauliflower
2 Tbsp butter
about 1 tsp curry powder
2 Tbsp flour
425g can Chunky Tomato and Onion
½–1 cup grated tasty cheese

Break cauliflower into 3cm-diameter florets and simmer until barely tender in lightly salted water, then drain and arrange in a baking dish in one layer.

While the cauliflower cooks, make the sauce. Heat the butter and curry powder until bubbling, stir in the flour, then the tomato mixture, and bring to the boil, stirring constantly. Thin with a little water if necessary, then pour evenly over the cauliflower. Sprinkle with as much cheese as you like, and put aside until needed.

Bake uncovered at 180°C, just until cheese melts and cauliflower heats through. Do not overcook.

Serve with chicken (pages 44–59) as part of a buffet or, alone, on rice.

SAVOURY BEANS AND TOMATOES

(See photograph page 70)
An interesting sauce like this gives new life to yet more beans from your garden!

250g green beans
1 large clove garlic
1 onion
2 Tbsp olive or other oil
1 Tbsp sugar
2 Tbsp wine vinegar
1 Tbsp grainy mustard
400g can whole tomatoes or 2 cups ripe
    cubed tomatoes
½ tsp salt
basil and/or sliced black olives (optional)

Trim beans and cut each diagonally into two or three, if large. Cook in a small amount of water in a covered pan.

Make sauce in another pot or pan. Chop garlic and onion, cover and cook in the oil until onion is tender, then add sugar, vinegar and mustard. Add tomatoes and salt and boil rapidly for 2–3 minutes, breaking tomatoes into smaller pieces as mixture boils down. Either add drained beans to sauce or serve sauce over drained beans.

Garnish with chopped basil and/or chopped black olives if available.

Serve with chicken (pages 44–59), fish (pages 28–41) or any unsauced 'vegetarian main'.

EGGPLANTS WITH PARSLEY AND GARLIC

In this recipe the vinegar makes all the difference to the flavour — it is really a subtle sweet-and-sour eggplant mixture.

For 6 servings:
2 medium-sized eggplants
salt
¼ cup olive oil
2 or 3 cloves of garlic, finely chopped
¼ cup chopped parsley
2 Tbsp capers
2 Tbsp caper vinegar
1 Tbsp sugar
about ¼ cup water
salt and freshly ground black pepper
extra parsley to garnish

Peel eggplants only if you think their skin is tough. Cut into 2cm slices. Sprinkle with salt and place into a large dish. Cover with paper towels and put another heavy dish on top of eggplants and allow to stand for 20 minutes.

Pat dry with fresh paper towels and cut the slices into cubes, or small pieces if you like.

Heat the oil in a large frypan. Toss eggplants and garlic in it. Cook over a medium heat for 15 minutes, turning several times. (The eggplants will absorb the oil fairly fast, but it is not essential to add more.) Add parsley, capers, caper vinegar and sugar. Cover and cook over a moderate heat for 5–10 minutes, adding more water if the eggplants dry out before they are tender.

Taste to check eggplants are tender, then adjust seasonings carefully, and sprinkle with extra parsley.

Serve hot or at room temperature, with barbecued or other plainly cooked chicken.

ROASTED RED ONION SALAD

Red onions are milder than other onions, they make an interesting and different salad.

For 4 servings:
4 red onions, quartered and roasted
    (page 57)
1 Tbsp olive oil
2 tsp wine vinegar
1 tsp balsamic vinegar
1 tsp sugar
½ tsp finely chopped fresh sage or thyme
    (optional)

Roast the quartered red onions without removing their roots, as in recipe for Roast Chicken Legs and Summer Vegetables (page 57).

While hot (or warm) transfer to a serving dish, sprinkle with remaining ingredients and turn lightly to coat, without breaking up the onions.

Serve warm or at room temperature (but not chilled) with barbecued foods.

VEGETABLES A LA GRECQUE

This is a lovely way to serve one vegetable, or a vegetable mixture, in the summer.

For 2–4 servings:
400–500g prepared vegetables
2 cloves garlic, chopped
¼ cup olive or other oil
2 Tbsp wine vinegar
1½ tsp coriander seeds, crushed
1 tsp sugar
½ tsp salt
425g can Mexican Spiced Tomatoes or
    Chunky Tomato and Onion
1 Tbsp lemon juice
¼ cup chopped parsley

Cut one or several types of vegetable into long strips or other neat pieces. Use carrots, beans, cauliflower, celery or zucchini.

Cook the garlic in the oil without browning it. Stir in the vinegar, the crushed coriander seeds, seasonings and the tomato mixture, then add the vegetables, cover and simmer for 10–15 minutes, or until tender-crisp, turning vegetables after 5 minutes.

Sprinkle with lemon juice and serve the

vegetables warm or cold, but preferably at room temperature, in their sauce, on a shallow dish, generously sprinkled with parsley.

Note:
Don't worry if green vegetables turn olive green. This is not because they are overcooked — the vinegar makes them change colour. They still taste fine!

Serve alone or with Roast Boned Chicken (page 58), and with plenty of crusty bread to mop up the delicious sauce.

79

▲ *Barbecued Fresh Vegetables*

BARBECUED FRESH VEGETABLES

Choose a colourful mixture of seasonal vegetables such as red onions, eggplants, zucchini, red and yellow peppers, etc. Cut them into chunky pieces. Quarter onions so pieces are held together by the root.

Brush with Seasoned Oil (below) and barbecue (or grill) about 12cm from the heat, turning frequently so vegetables cook before they burn. Allow vegetables to brown but not burn on their edges.

Seasoned Oil:
½ cup olive oil
2 cloves garlic, peeled
6 basil leaves, chopped
2 Tbsp fresh thyme
2 Tbsp fresh rosemary

Put all ingredients in a food processor fitted with its metal chopping blade. Process until finely chopped. Allow to stand for at least 10 minutes then strain, discarding flavourings.

Serve with Red-Cooked Chicken (see page 50).

80

PASTA SALAD

(See photograph pages 76–77.)
Pasta salads are popular but, unfortunately, often they do not taste as good as they look. By making a strongly flavoured dressing we hope we have overcome this.

For 4–6 servings:
250g tortellini, spirals, or other pasta
    shapes
1 Tbsp oil
½ cup tomato purée
2 Tbsp sour cream
¼–½ cup olive oil
1 Tbsp wine vinegar
1 tsp sugar
½ tsp salt
1 tsp cumin
½ tsp oreganum, crumbled
Optional:
1 or 2 firm tomatoes, diced
2 spring onions, thinly sliced white and
    green parts
2 Tbsp finely chopped parsley
1 stalk celery, sliced thinly
¼–½ cup small cubes of unpeeled
    telegraph cucumber
½ cup drained whole-kernel corn

Cook the pasta until just tender in plenty of boiling, lightly salted water with the tablespoon of oil, then drain it thoroughly. Take care not to undercook or overcook the pasta, if you want a good salad.

Mix together the next eight ingredients, using olive oil for its flavour if possible. Stir the dressing gently into the hot, drained pasta, and allow to stand for at least 15 minutes. During this time the pasta will absorb a lot of the dressing. Refrigerate the salad until you want to serve it.

Just before serving add the tomatoes, spring onions, and any other optional ingredients, and stir into the salad.

Serve with grilled or barbecued chicken, or as part of a buffet meal.

EGGPLANT KEBABS

Eggplant that is marinated in the mixture below makes a good accompaniment for food from any part of the world.

For 4 servings:
200g eggplant, cut into cubes
2 cloves garlic, finely chopped
¼ cup olive oil
2 Tbsp sesame oil
2 Tbsp wine vinegar
1 Tbsp light soya sauce
1 tsp honey
1 tsp grated fresh ginger
½ tsp salt

Combine all ingredients except eggplant in a jar, or using a food processor or blender, and use to marinate cubed eggplant for about 30 minutes. Thread eggplant pieces onto medium-length skewers that have been soaked in cold water.

Grill or barbecue until cut flesh is evenly golden, turning frequently, about

10 minutes. Brush with extra marinade during cooking.

Serve hot, or at room temperature, with grilled or barbecued fish or chicken.

ROASTED PEPPER SALAD

(See photograph pages 76–77.)
Peppers prepared like this have a wonderful flavour and an interesting texture. They are really like a different vegetable.

4–6 plump, fleshy red, green, yellow or
    orange peppers
¼ cup lemon juice
¼ cup olive oil
freshly ground black pepper

Use fresh, firm and fleshy peppers. Heat whole peppers under a grill, over a barbecue rack, or on a gas burner, keeping them close to the heat, and turning them as their skin blisters and blackens. Or roast in an oven heated to 220°C for about 30 minutes.

When they have blackened in patches and have blistered fairly evenly, put then in a paper or plastic bag to stand for 5–10 minutes, then hold them, one at a time, under a cold tap and peel or cut off the skin. The flesh underneath should be brightly coloured and partly cooked.

Quarter the peppers, and trim away the seeds and pith. Cut into even shapes, put them in a shallow dish, and coat with the lemon juice and oil, using less or more, depending on the amount of flesh you have. Refrigerate until you need them, up to two days.

Sprinkle with freshly ground pepper and serve at room temperature.

Serve as a separate starter course, or as a vegetable alongside chicken. These are especially good with other Mediterranean recipes.

FRIGGIONE

Do not hurry the cooking time of this recipe. Although it loses its bright colour, it tastes better and better as the liquid disappears and the mixture browns.

For 4–6 servings:
about ¼ cup olive oil
4 large potatoes
2 large red onions
2 red or green peppers
425g can Italian Seasoned Tomatoes
1–1½ tsp salt
1 tsp sugar
freshly ground black pepper
chopped parsley (optional)

Heat the oil in a large frypan, preferably one with a non-stick surface. Add potatoes cut into small cubes, and the onions and peppers, cut into strips or rings. Cover and cook over a moderate heat for 20 minutes, stirring several times, until the vegetables are tender and lightly browned.

Add the tomatoes and their juice. Cook uncovered, over a medium heat for 20–25 minutes, until the mixture darkens in colour and has reduced, so there is only a small amount of liquid around the potatoes. Season to taste.

Serve warm or hot, reheating in the frypan if necessary. Sprinkle with parsley. Excellent alone or as part of a barbecue or buffet meal.

SPICY RICE PILAF

This is a very tasty alternative to plainly cooked rice.

For 4 servings:
2 Tbsp oil
1 medium onion, finely chopped
2 cloves garlic, finely chopped
¼ cup whole or slivered almonds
1 cup long grain rice
1 medium carrot, finely diced
¼ cup dried currants or sultanas
½ tsp each ground cumin, coriander, cinnamon and chilli powder
¼ tsp ground cloves
grated rind of 1 lemon or orange
3 cups (boiling) vegetable or chicken stock (or 3 cups water plus 3 tsp instant stock)

Heat the oil in a large frypan (or flameproof casserole dish), and cook the onions and garlic over a moderate heat, for about 2 minutes. Add the almonds and cook until lightly browned.

Stir in the rice, diced carrot, currants and the spices and cook for a few minutes longer, stirring frequently. Add the grated citrus rind and the stock.

Bring mixture to the boil, cover and simmer gently for about 15 minutes until rice is cooked and liquid is absorbed.

Or bake, covered with a close-fitting lid or foil, at 170°C for 1 hour.

Or microwave in a covered dish on Medium High (70% power) for about 15 minutes.

Serve with Moroccan Chicken (page 54) or any Middle Eastern type foods.

RICE SALAD

Rice makes substantial salads, to which small amounts of vegetables may be added for flavour and texture contrast.

For 4–6 servings:
2–3 cups cooked brown or white rice
1 or 2 carrots, shredded
1 or 2 sticks celery, thinly sliced
about 6 radishes, thinly sliced
2 or 3 spring onions, thinly sliced
¼ cup chopped parsley

Dressing:
½ cup oil
¼ cup wine or cider vinegar
1 Tbsp mixed mustard
2 tsp sugar
1 tsp salt

Make this salad with leftover or freshly cooked rice. (Leave freshly cooked rice to stand for at least 10 minutes then toss lightly with a fork to separate the grains.)

Fold into the rice the shredded carrot, thinly sliced celery and radishes, and the thinly sliced spring onions. Add the chopped parsley and any other fresh herbs you have and like.

Shake the remaining ingredients together in a screw-topped jar. Toss about half this dressing through the salad, stopping when you like the flavour. As rice absorbs much of the dressing, add more before serving, for best flavour.

Variations:
• For Peanutty Rice Salad add chopped sultanas, and chopped roasted peanuts with the carrot. Mix enough sesame oil into the dressing to give it a nutty flavour.
• Add sweet chilli sauce for hotness and extra sweetness.

Serve as part of a buffet or picnic meal, with your favourite chicken dish.

Mediterranean Potatoes ▲

MEDITERRANEAN POTATOES

*It takes only a little effort to turn everyday potatoes into something that will
delight everybody who eats them.*

For 2 main servings:
about 800g good-quality potatoes
2–3 Tbsp olive or other oil
1 or 2 large cloves garlic, very finely
*   chopped*
chilli powder or cayenne pepper
several sprigs of fresh thyme, rosemary or
*   sage*
salt or 2 tsp capers
2 tsp chopped anchovies
2 tsp caper vinegar
about ¼ cup chopped parsley
black olives (optional)

Scrub the potatoes with a soft brush to
remove all dirt, then cut lengthways into
large chunky wedges or chip shapes.
Rinse in cold water, and pat dry.

Heat the oil in a large heavy frypan.
Add the potatoes, tossing in the oil to
coat. Cover, and cook, turning every 5
minutes for about 20 minutes, until
potatoes are barely tender, and are
lightly browned on most sides. While
turning the second time, add the garlic,
sprinkle the potatoes with chilli powder
or cayenne pepper then mix well. Put

several sprigs of your chosen herb and
the salt or capers on top of the potatoes.

As soon as the potatoes are tender,
remove the herbs, add the anchovies
and caper vinegar and cook for about
10 minutes longer, uncovered, turning
occasionally.

Mix in the chopped parsley just before
serving. Scatter the olives over the top.

*Serve bowls of warm or hot potatoes with
poached eggs and Spinach Salad (page
86).*

83

▲ *Left to right: 'Taste of the Tropics' Salad, Kumara Salad, Harlequin Salad*

'TASTE OF THE TROPICS' SALAD

The dressing on this salad is wonderful! It is particularly good on avocados and pawpaws, which have a melting texture, but is worth trying with other ripe fruit.

1 avocado
½ pawpaw (papaya)
1 small red onion
¼ cup roasted peanuts, chopped coarsely
Dressing:
2 Tbsp slivered basil leaves
2 tsp lime juice
2 tsp lemon juice
2 Tbsp fish sauce
1 Tbsp honey
1 Tbsp Thai chilli sauce

Deseed and peel the avocado and pawpaw, and cube or cut in small wedges. Add the finely chopped onion and the coarsely chopped peanuts.

Combine all dressing ingredients in a screw-topped jar and shake well. Gently toss about half the dressing through the salad, taking care not to break up the

avocado and papaya. Taste and add more if you think it necessary.

Serve with plain chicken and fish dishes, to add unusual flavour and lovely colour.

HARLEQUIN SALAD

This colourful salad is brought to life by its interesting dressing.

1 carrot
½ green pepper
½ red pepper
1 medium-sized red onion
440g can whole-kernel corn

Dressing:
2 Tbsp grated root ginger
3 Tbsp fresh coriander leaves, chopped
¼ cup chopped chives
½ cup olive oil
¼ cup balsamic or sherry vinegar
2 tsp light soya sauce
1 tsp dry mustard
½ tsp salt
½ tsp (Thai) sweet chilli sauce
½ tsp finely grated orange peel
¼ tsp black pepper

Peel the carrot and cut into thin shreds. Halve the green and red peppers, discard seeds and pith, and cut peppers into thin shreds. Slice the onion into very thin rings. Try to have all the long thin pieces about the same length.

Combine the shredded vegetables with the drained corn.

When you are ready to serve the salad, toss dressing through the vegetables, using as much as you like.

Combine all ingredients for dressing, shake well in a screw-topped jar or mix using a food processor.

Serve with Rice Salad (page 82) or Pasta Salad (page 81) as part of a picnic or buffet meal.

KUMARA SALAD

Try this salad with and without the dressing and, if you like, leave out some of the additions.

3 kumara (750g)
¼ cup sultanas
1 firm banana
¼–½ cup flaked coconut
1 can mandarin segments (optional)
1 green pepper, chopped
2 spring onions, finely chopped

Dressing:
½ cup olive or other oil
¼ cup white wine vinegar
1 tsp mixed mustard
1–2 tsp grated root ginger
½ tsp salt
1 tsp honey or brown sugar

Cook the scrubbed kumara in a covered container in the microwave oven until tender. When they are cool enough to handle, peel and chop into bite-sized pieces.

Put the sultanas into a sieve and pour boiling water over them to plump them up a little, then drain well. Mix through the kumara.

Slice the banana, and add with the coconut, drained mandarin segments, pepper, and spring onions to the kumara and sultanas.

Combine all dressing ingredients in a screw-topped jar and shake well.

Toss all the salad ingredients gently with about half of the dressing, adding the remainder just before serving.

Serve alone with freshly made Bread Rolls (page 104) or with plain chicken or fish.

POTATO SALAD WITH LEMON MAYONNAISE

With homemade mayonnaise used as one of the main ingredients, this potato salad is wonderful. Alter flavourings to suit yourself.

For 4–6 servings:
about 1 kg small new potatoes
3 eggs, hard-boiled
½ cup Mayonnaise (page 115)
2 Tbsp lemon juice
1–2 Tbsp chopped tarragon, basil, spring
    onions or parsley (optional)

Quarter or halve the potatoes lengthways, and boil or microwave until just cooked, adding water as required. Hard-boil the eggs with the potatoes if desired.

Drain the potatoes and leave to cool. If you are making the mayonnaise, use lemon juice rather than vinegar. Measure out ½ cup of mayonnaise and add the extra lemon juice and chopped herbs.

Peel the eggs, then chop two of them. In a large bowl toss together the cooled potatoes, the mayonnaise and the chopped egg.

Pile into a serving bowl and garnish by finely grating the remaining egg over the top. Refrigerate until required.

Serve with a leafy green salad as part of a summer meal.

MIXED GREEN SALAD

Our mixed green salads are different every time we make them, as they are made from such a wide variety of salad vegetables.

Choose from:
young lettuce leaves
iceberg lettuce, chopped
young spinach leaves
young nasturtium leaves
lambs lettuce leaves
young celery leaves
watercress leaves
snow pea shoots
mild onion rings
cucumber, sliced thinly
green peppers
rocket leaves
mustard and cress
spring onions, sliced
avocado slices

Prepare a selection of the leaves listed at left. For best results after removing damaged parts, stems, etc., wash by immersing in a sink or container of cold water (so grit etc. falls to the bottom, away from the leaves). Shake to remove most of the water, or lie leaves on a clean, dry teatowel or a long length of paper towels. Roll up like a sponge roll and refrigerate until needed (up to 12 hours).

Just before serving, tip dried, chilled leaves into a salad bowl, dribble with your selected dressing (page 89), then toss to coat leaves lightly and evenly.

Serve with any vegetarian, poultry or fish dish, for lunch or dinner.

SPINACH SALAD

Spinach salad is a special treat. In warm weather you can happily eat a large shallow bowlful as a complete meal.

For 4 large or 6 small servings:
400–500g spinach
200g button mushrooms
a few water chestnuts (optional)
Croutons (page 112)
avocado (optional)
½ cup toasted pinenuts

Dressing:
¼ cup olive oil
about ¼ tsp salt
1 tsp sugar
2–3 tsp Dijon-type mustard
2 Tbsp wine vinegar

Wash and drain the spinach, then break the large leaves off the stems, leaving the central rib attached to the stem (so each leaf is in two halves lengthways). Leave small leaves whole. Handle leaves carefully to avoid bruising. Roll in a teatowel and refrigerate, making sure that the leaves are cold and dry before they are used in the salad.

Wash, dry and slice the mushrooms. Drain canned water chestnuts and slice them.

Make Croutons (page 112).

Just before serving slice avocado then put the cold dry spinach, mushrooms,

water chestnuts and sliced avocado in a large serving bowl or plastic bag, pour the dressing over and toss gently until the vegetables are coated. Arrange attractively in individual bowls and sprinkle generously with toasted pinenuts and croutons.

To make the dressing:
Mix the oil with the salt, sugar, mustard and vinegar and leave it to stand at room temperature until the salad is required.

Serve immediately, alone as a separate course or teamed with a plainly cooked main course.

MEDITERRANEAN SALAD

This is like a Greek salad with extra 'goodies' added.

For 4 side servings:
100g assorted lettuce leaves
1 red pepper, diced
1 green pepper, diced
6–8 small tomatoes, quartered
½–1 cup cucumber, cubed
50–70g feta cheese, cubed
20 black olives
4–6 anchovy fillets (optional)

Dressing:
2 Tbsp olive oil
2 Tbsp lemon juice
1 tsp prepared mustard
1–2 Tbsp chopped fresh herbs (e.g. basil, parsley, oreganum, thyme)
salt and pepper

Arrange the washed lettuce leaves in the bottom of four bowls. Prepare then toss together the next six ingredients, and arrange over the lettuce. Chop the anchovy fillets over the salads.

Combine all the dressing ingredients in a screw-topped jar, and shake until opaque.

Drizzle dressing evenly over the salads just before serving.

Serve with Mediterranean Potatoes (page 83) or with plainly cooked poultry.

CAESAR SALAD

Here is our version of this popular dish.
It is important that it is made with crisp lettuce leaves.

For 4–6 servings:
1 cos (romaine) lettuce
½–1 cup Croutons (page 112)
½ cup freshly grated parmesan cheese

Dressing:
1 egg
1 clove garlic
juice of 1 lime or lemon
2 anchovy fillets
1 tsp Dijon mustard
½ tsp Worcestershire sauce
½ cup extra virgin olive oil
about ½ tsp salt
freshly ground black pepper

Separate and wash lettuce leaves, then dry well. Chill for several hours, or overnight. Leaves should be cold and dry when the salad is made.

To assemble the salad: Arrange the leaves in a large salad bowl, sprinkling the croutons through them. Just before serving, drizzle the dressing through and around the leaves, toss carefully to coat leaves with dressing, then sprinkle with freshly grated parmesan cheese.

To make the dressing, combine all ingredients except the oil in a food processor bowl. Blend until smooth,

then, while the motor is still running, pour the olive oil in a slow, steady stream until the dressing is the consistency of thick pouring cream. Taste and adjust the seasonings.

Variation:
Make dressing exactly as above but without the egg.

A salad as good as this may be served alone as a course by itself, or with plainly grilled or barbecued meat.

▲ *Left to right: Herbed Vinaigrette, Peanutty Dressing, Tomato Dressing, Basil Mayonnaise*

SALAD DRESSINGS

*Be adventurous with the salad dressings that follow. Use them to add zing and
zest to a variety of plainly cooked hot or cold vegetables, meats and poultry!
Try dressings with all sorts of salad vegetables and with ripe fruits in season.
Many of our salad dressings are made with olive oil, which although it adds
delicious flavour, is not essential and can be replaced by other salad oils. If you
do use olive oil, make sure you bring dressings to room temperature before
serving, as olive oil solidifies on refrigeration.*

Herbed Vinaigrette

¾ cup olive oil
¼ cup wine vinegar
1 tsp mixed mustard
3–4 Tbsp chopped fresh herbs
1 clove garlic, finely chopped
½ tsp salt
½ tsp sugar
pepper to taste

Put all ingredients into a food processor or blender and process until well combined, or shake well in a screw-topped jar.

Refrigerate in a covered container, for up to two weeks.

Use on raw vegetables, or hot or cold cooked vegetables, especially green beans, potatoes, tomatoes, and leafy salad vegetables, button mushrooms, raw red/green peppers, shredded cabbage, cooked cauliflower and broccoli. Shake well before using.

Basil Mayonnaise

Make our basic Mayonnaise (page 115), adding 6–8 large basil leaves before processing.

Good on almost any plainly cooked hot or cold food. Try on coleslaw, potato salad, hard-boiled eggs, cold chicken, baked potatoes or apple and celery salad.

Italian Dressing

2 tsp cornflour
½ cup water
2–3 tsp onion pulp
1 small clove garlic, finely chopped
1 tsp dried oreganum, crumbled
1 tsp mixed mustard
½ tsp paprika
1 tsp salt
1 Tbsp sugar
1 Tbsp tomato paste
¼ cup wine vinegar
½ cup olive or other oil

Mix together the cornflour and water in a small pot and bring to the boil, stirring until thick. Cool slightly and put into a screw-topped jar with the remaining ingredients. Shake until well combined.

Refrigerate for up to a month. Shake well before use.

Especially good on leafy salad vegetables, warm potatoes, cold cooked beans and baby carrots, lightly cooked asparagus, raw mushrooms, tomatoes, raw or cooked peppers, shredded carrot, cold roasted peppers, or as a dressing for avocados.

Peanutty Dressing

3 Tbsp crunchy peanut butter
2 cloves garlic
2 Tbsp light soya sauce
2 Tbsp wine vinegar
1 Tbsp brown sugar or runny honey
1 Tbsp sesame oil
1 tsp Tabasco sauce
about ¼ cup very hot water

Put all ingredients except the hot water into a food processor or blender. Process until well combined. Thin down to pouring cream consistency with very hot water.

Refrigerate for up to two weeks, warming before use if necessary.

Especially good over hot or cold kumara or potatoes, brushed over chicken before grilling. Toss through warm pasta or noodles, cooked chicken, cooked julienne vegetables. Add to cooked rice.

Strawberry Vinaigrette

½ cup mashed fresh strawberries
¼ cup olive oil
¼ cup other salad oil
1 tsp sugar
¼ tsp Tabasco sauce
pinch of salt
2 Tbsp wine or raspberry vinegar
1 tsp balsamic vinegar

Hull and wash strawberries, and mash lightly with a fork before measuring. Put the mashed strawberries and all other ingredients into a food processor and process until well combined.

Best used the day it is made. Serve over avocado, smoked chicken, smoked salmon, or crisp young lettuce leaves.

Tomato Dressing

2 spring onions, chopped
½ cup tomato purée
3 Tbsp wine vinegar
2 tsp mixed mustard
2 tsp sugar
½ tsp salt
1 cup olive or other oil

Combine all ingredients in a screw-topped jar, shake until well combined. Refrigerate for up to a week. Shake well before using.

Use on avocados, hot or warm green beans, hot or cold asparagus, plainly cooked mussels, warm zucchini, shredded carrot, coleslaw, or cooked cauliflower.

Variation:
Add chopped coriander leaves, if available.

Parmesan Dressing

¼ cup olive or other oil
1 Tbsp wine or herb vinegar
1 tsp mixed mustard
1 clove garlic, finely chopped
¼ tsp salt
2 Tbsp grated parmesan cheese

Shake all ingredients in a screw-topped jar.

Brush on bread or any vegetables, especially flat mushrooms, zucchini, eggplant before grilling (See Mushroom and Avocado Melt page 74). Toss through sautéed potatoes, use on salad greens, diced raw apples or pears, pour over plainly cooked carrots, or green vegetables before serving.

Lemon Honey Dressing

¼ cup lemon juice
2 Tbsp light soya sauce
2 Tbsp salad oil
2 Tbsp honey
1 Tbsp Dijon mustard
1 Tbsp sesame oil
1 tsp finely grated lemon rind
1 clove garlic, finely chopped

Combine all ingredients and either process until smooth using a food processor, or shake well in a screw-topped jar.

Very good over diced fresh fruit, such as apples, pears, peaches, nectarines, etc. Use over finely shredded raw vegetables, or lightly cooked stir-fried asparagus, green beans or other vegetables.

Sesame Dressing

2 cloves garlic, finely chopped
1 tsp grated fresh ginger
1 Tbsp dark soya sauce
1 Tbsp light soya sauce
1 tsp sesame oil
2 tsp sugar
2 tsp rice vinegar
*2 Tbsp finely chopped fresh coriander
   leaves*

Combine all ingredients in a screw-topped jar and shake well to combine.

Serve over stir-fried vegetables, as a dipping sauce for plainly cooked chicken or fish, or with grilled vegetables such as eggplant, zucchini, or red peppers.

From top to bottom: yoghurt, Toasted Coconut, Cucumber in Yoghurt, Lentil Dahl (page 19), Herbed Tomatoes (page 91)

CURRY ACCOMPANIMENTS

Microwaved Rice

Microwaved rice never burns or sticks and may be left to finish cooking while you are out of the house. Put 1 cup of basmati, jasmine, parcooked or long-grain rice in a large microwave dish with 2¼ cups boiling water, ½ tsp salt and 1 Tbsp oil (if you like). Cover loosely with lid ajar or with plastic cling film. Microwave for 12 minutes on Medium (50% power), then allow to stand for 5 minutes, before serving. Reheat if necessary. (Rice cooked on High [100% power] takes the same time but is much more likely to boil over.)

Foolproof Boiled Rice

This is a good way to cook rice if you do not have a microwave oven, or a heavy bottomed pot with a close-fitting lid. (Aromatic, basmati and jasmine rice lose some flavour cooked by this method.) Bring 6 cups water to the boil in a large pot. Add 1 tsp salt and 1 Tbsp oil then sprinkle in 1 cup long-grain rice. Boil uncovered for 12–15 minutes, until a grain of rice, when squeezed between the finger and thumb, has no hard core and breaks into two pieces. Drain through a sieve and keep hot or reheat when needed, standing the sieve over a pot of boiling water with a lid or foil over it.

Poppadoms

Spray poppadoms with non-stick spray and microwave on High (100% power), one at a time on a folded paper towel for 40–70 seconds, until puffed over the whole surface.

Toasted Sesame Seeds

Toast sesame seeds by tipping them into a large frypan and heating over low-to-moderate heat, shaking often, until lightly and evenly browned. Use immediately or store in an airtight jar.

90

Toasted Coconut

Spread fine or medium desiccated coconut or shredded coconut in a sponge-roll tin. Heat under a low grill or in a moderate oven until the coconut is lightly browned. Watch carefully as coconut browns and burns quickly.

Chopped Roasted Peanuts

Buy good quality roasted peanuts, chop coarsely, and serve alone, with Banana Raita (below), or with sliced cooked kumara in plain yoghurt or Spicy Yoghurt Sauce (below).

Banana Raita

Slice fairly firm bananas and sprinkle with lemon or orange juice to stop them browning. Fold plain yoghurt (using quantities to suit your own taste) through the banana. Add cinnamon, chopped mint, chopped coriander leaves, chopped peanuts or toasted sesame seeds, if you like.

Cucumber in Yoghurt

Thinly slice or coarsely grate an unpeeled (telegraph) cucumber. Sprinkle with a teaspoon of salt, mix gently, allow to stand for 10 minutes, then rinse with cold water and drain. Make a dressing by mixing $\frac{1}{2}$ cup plain, unsweetened yoghurt, the juice of $\frac{1}{2}$ lemon, a small crushed garlic clove, and about $\frac{1}{4}$ teaspoon finely grated fresh root ginger. Mix the cucumber and dressing about 10 minutes before serving.

Wilted Cucumber Salad

Halve a telegraph cucumber lengthways. Scoop out the seeds using a small teaspoon. Cut in thin slices and stand these in brine made from 1 tsp salt and 1 cup water for 10 minutes. Drain and pat slices dry. Mix with 2 chopped spring onions, 1 small clove garlic (optional), 2 Tbsp wine vinegar, a pinch of chilli powder and 1 Tbsp of toasted sesame seeds (see page 90) crushed with 1 tsp sugar in a pestle and mortar. Refrigerate.

Kiwifruit Salsa

4 ripe kiwifruit, chopped or sliced
$\frac{1}{4}$ cup finely sliced spring onion or
*   shallots*
$\frac{1}{4}$ red pepper, chopped
1 clove garlic, finely chopped
$\frac{1}{2}$ cup basil leaves, finely chopped
$\frac{1}{4}$ tsp very finely chopped red or green
*   chilli (without seeds)*
1 tsp ground cumin
$\frac{1}{4}$ cup lime juice
salt
freshly ground black pepper

Combine all the ingredients, tossing gently together so the kiwifruit keeps its shape. Refrigerate for up to 24 hours in a covered container.

Note:
Take care when you use fresh chillies. It is very hard to tell exactly how hot some small fresh chillies are. Mixtures containing thinly sliced chilli get hotter on standing. If in doubt, use a pinch of chilli powder or a teaspoonful of Tabasco sauce.

Variation:
Replace the kiwifruit with any other fresh raw fruit such as melons, pears, pineapples, peaches, etc.

Spiced Cabbage with Coconut

2 Tbsp butter or oil
1 onion or 4 shallots
2 cloves garlic, chopped
$\frac{1}{2}$ tsp whole cumin seeds
1 tsp ground cumin
$\frac{1}{2}$ tsp turmeric
1 small or $\frac{1}{2}$ large cabbage, shredded
$\frac{1}{4}$ cup desiccated coconut
$\frac{1}{4}$ cup water
1–2 tsp cornflour (optional)

Put the butter or oil in a large frypan, add the sliced onion or shallots, the garlic and the whole cumin seeds, and cook on moderate heat until the onion is transparent but not browned. Stir in the ground cumin and turmeric and cook for about 1 minute longer.

Add the cabbage, coconut and water, turn to coat the cabbage with the spices, cover and cook over fairly high heat for 5–10 minutes, until the cabbage is tender-crisp and nearly all the liquid has evaporated. Serve like this, or mix the cornflour to a paste with about a tablespoon of water, and stir it into the cabbage to thicken the remaining liquid. Turn the cabbage so that it is coated with the lightly thickened sauce and serve straight away.

Variation:
Add a little chilli powder when you add the ground cumin and turmeric.

Herbed Tomatoes

Slice or cut 3 or 4 ripe red tomatoes into chunks or wedges. Toss with 2 or 3 finely chopped spring onions, about 2 Tbsp of finely chopped mint, basil, or coriander leaves, the juice of a lemon, about 1 tsp sugar, $\frac{1}{4}$–$\frac{1}{2}$ tsp salt and a few drops Tabasco sauce. Cover and refrigerate for 15–30 minutes. Turn to coat tomatoes with the dressing before serving.

Carrot Chutney

Shred 2 fairly large carrots coarsely. Mix with them 1 finely chopped spring onion, 3–4 tsp finely chopped mint, about 1 tsp finely grated ginger, and 2 Tbsp lemon juice. Refrigerate in a plastic bag for up to two days.

Variation:
Add $\frac{1}{2}$ cup chopped sultanas.

Spicy Yoghurt Sauce

Delicious spooned over dahl, sliced bananas or cucumber, or stirred through shredded coconut.

1 large clove garlic
1 small fresh green chilli
$\frac{1}{4}$ cup chopped fresh coriander leaves
2 spring onions, chopped
1 tsp ground cumin
$\frac{1}{2}$ tsp sugar
$\frac{1}{2}$ tsp salt
1 cup plain, unsweetened yoghurt

Put all the ingredients except the yoghurt in a food processor and process until finely chopped. Add the yoghurt and process until mixed, or chop the vegetables very finely, then stir into the remaining ingredients.

Fresh Fruit Salsa

A fruit salsa like this is a cross between a salad and a relish.

2 cups diced or sliced ripe mango,
*   peaches, nectarines, pawpaw, etc.*
2–3 Tbsp lime juice
2 Tbsp finely chopped coriander leaves
*   or mint*
about $\frac{1}{2}$ tsp very finely chopped fresh
*   green chilli or 1 tsp Tabasco sauce*
$\frac{1}{2}$ tsp salt

Slice or dice the fruit into an unpunctured plastic bag. Add the lime juice and the remaining ingredients. Toss gently to coat the fruit. Refrigerate until required.

Breakfasts

What's for breakfast? Different people have different ideas about the foods they consider suitable for breakfast.

There are those who like to follow the same routine and eat exactly the same food every morning, while others will happily polish off whatever happens to be sitting on the bench or in the refrigerator, left over from any meal from the previous day!

It's hard to beat cereal, fruit and (reduced-fat) milk or yoghurt for a breakfast which is nutritionally well balanced and quick to prepare and eat. Try some of our favourite porridge recipes in cool weather, and our interesting muesli recipes if you want something new and different in your cereal bowls.

And, so you can get weekends off to a good start, we have included several of our favourite breakfast pancake, waffle and french toast recipes!

Whatever you do, don't get into the habit of forgetting breakfast, or deciding you can do without it — none of us function 'on all cylinders' without something in our stomachs at the start of the day. What's more, snacks bought mid-morning, when hunger pangs strike, are expensive, and often not as good for us as our regular breakfast.

◀ **Oaty Pancakes (page 97)**

MIXED-GRAIN APPLE PORRIDGE

Keep a selection of kibbled and flaked grains in jars, to make a variety of mixed-grain porridges quickly and easily. Add dried fruits for more variety.

For 2 servings:

3 Tbsp wholegrain rolled oats
3 Tbsp kibbled wheat or kibbled rye
3 Tbsp wheatgerm or wheatbran
3 Tbsp chopped dried apple
3 tsp Cinnamon Sugar
1¾ cups hot water
pinch of salt

Combine the cereals, apple and Cinnamon Sugar (see below) in a microwavable jug or deep bowl. Pour in the hot water, add the salt, and stir to mix. Microwave for 1 minute on High (100% power). Stir the porridge, then cook for 4–6 minutes on Medium (50% power), until the grains are tender. Keep an eye on the porridge, adding more hot water if it looks dry. Stir as desired.

Briefly stirred porridge has a grainy texture, and frequently stirred cereal is pastier.

Cinnamon Sugar

Shake together then store in a screw-topped jar ¼ cup of brown sugar, ¼ cup of white sugar, and 1 Tbsp of cinnamon.

Serve with milk or plain or fruity yoghurt.

WARM CRUNCHY CEREAL

Cooked seeds, dried fruit and nuts give this nutritious cereal a unique and pleasing texture. You may find you like it so much that you cook (or reheat) it at any time of the day!

For 2 servings:

½ cup wholegrain rolled oats
2 Tbsp pumpkin or sunflower seeds
1–2 Tbsp chopped dried apricots
1–2 Tbsp chopped or flaked almonds
1–2 Tbsp sultanas
1½ cups hot water

Put first five ingredients into a microwavable jug or deep bowl or into a pot on the stove. Pour in the hot water and stir to mix well. Microwave on High (100% power) for 4–5 minutes, stirring after 1 and 3 minutes, or simmer on the stovetop for 5–10 minutes, until

the porridge is the texture you like. Stir before serving, adding a little extra water if too thick.

Serve warm rather than very hot with milk, yoghurt and sliced bananas. Add a little sugar or golden syrup if you like.

MALTED SWISS MUESLI

You won't believe how good this is until you try it! It's easy, delicious, and always popular. The malted milk gives it a special character of its own.

For 2 servings:

1 large apple, coarsely chopped
about ¼ cup orange juice
½ cup fine or coarse rolled oats
¼ cup shredded coconut
2–3 Tbsp lightly toasted flaked almonds
¼ cup malted milk powder (Horlicks)

Put the unpeeled, roughly sliced apple with the orange juice in a food processor and process in short bursts until the apple is cut into chunky, even pieces. Add the rolled oats, coconut, almonds and malted milk powder. Process again very briefly to dampen these ingredients without chopping the apple too finely. Add a little extra juice

if mixture is too thick.

Variation:

If you do not have malted milk powder, add more orange juice or some fruit-flavoured yoghurt instead.

Pile into bowls and serve immediately with your favourite fruit-flavoured yoghurt and fresh fruit if you like.

MUNCHY MUESLI

This muesli contains many 'goodies', has the right amount of crunch and tastes great!

For 16 servings:

2 cups wholegrain oats
¼ cup wheatgerm
¼ cup oatbran or fibre-rich bran
¼ cup fine or medium coconut
¼ cup pumpkin seeds
¼ cup sunflower seeds
¼ cup sliced almonds
¼ cup honey
2 Tbsp sugar
¼ tsp salt
1 Tbsp water
2 Tbsp canola or other oil
½ cup chopped dried fruit (apricots, apples, pears, sultanas, raisins)

Mix the first seven ingredients together in a large bowl. Heat together the honey, sugar, salt, water and oil in a pot or microwave dish, stirring until the sugar has dissolved. Pour hot liquid over the dry mixture and stir to mix. Spread the mixture in a large, shallow baking pan and bake at 150°C for 20 minutes or until lightly browned. Stir if edges darken.

Or: spread the mixture on a microwave turntable, leaving centre uncovered. Microwave uncovered, on High (100% power) for 6–10 minutes, or until lightly browned, checking after about 4 minutes, and turning if necessary, to make sure mixture is browning evenly. Add dried fruits. Cool and store in an airtight container.

Serve with fresh or stewed fruit and yoghurt or milk.

From top to bottom: Mixed-Grain Apple Porridge, ▶
Warm Crunchy Cereal, Malted Swiss Muesli

PAIN PERDU

When stale bread is dipped in an orange-flavoured custard mixture, then cooked gently on a hot surface until it has puffed up and is golden brown, it turns into something wonderful — a variation on French Toast.

For 4 servings:
2 eggs
½ cup milk
2 Tbsp orange juice
1 tsp grated orange rind
2 Tbsp sugar
1 tsp vanilla
pinch of salt
1 Tbsp orange liqueur (optional)
8 slices french bread, each cut
    diagonally, 1cm thick

Place all ingredients except french bread in a bowl, and whisk until well mixed. (Add the liqueur for special occasions.) Place the bread in a large, shallow dish and cover with the egg mixture. Leave for 20–30 minutes, turning occasionally.

Heat a little butter in a large frypan. Add the bread and cook over low heat for 5–10 minutes a side, turning when golden brown.

Serve immediately, topped with berries, a dusting of icing sugar, and a trickle of maple syrup, or serve with jam or jelly.

OATY PANCAKES

(See photograph pages 92–93.)
Many people that turn up their noses at rolled oats porridge can't get enough of these pancakes, which contain a generous amount of the same oats!

For 3–4 servings:
¾ cup milk
¾ cup rolled oats
1 egg
½ tsp salt
2–3 Tbsp sugar
½ cup self-raising flour
25g butter, melted

Pour the milk over the rolled oats in a large mixing bowl, add the rest of the ingredients and mix with a fork (or food processor) just enough to combine.

Heat a lightly buttered or sprayed frypan or griddle to 180°C, or until a drop of water on the heated surface breaks up into several droplets that dance around the pan. Shape the pancakes onto the heated surface and cook until bubbles form and burst on the surface of the

pancake. Slide a thin metal blade under the pancake and flip it over. Cook the second side until the centre springs back when pressed. Adjust heat if necessary, until pancakes are golden when these stages are reached.

Stack several hot pancakes, top with a little butter (so that it melts over the pancakes) and serve with maple or golden syrup or honey.

PINEAPPLE WAFFLES

This waffle mixture may also be cooked as pancakes or pikelets. All three versions of the recipe are well worth trying — they have such a good flavour they don't really need any syrup over them.

For 3–4 servings:
2 Tbsp butter
2 Tbsp sugar
1 egg
¼ cup milk
225g can crushed pineapple
1 cup self-raising flour

Melt the butter in a bowl or pot big enough to mix everything. Add the sugar, egg, milk and the contents of the can of pineapple. Beat lightly with a fork to combine all ingredients. Fold in the flour, mixing just enough to combine the two mixtures — do not overmix. Heat a waffle iron according to the manufacturer's instructions. Spray with non-stick spray. Pour the batter

into the prepared iron. Close the lid and cook at a moderate heat for 4–5 minutes, until evenly cooked and golden brown. (Cook longer at a lower temperature for crisper waffles.)

Serve warm or hot, plain or with fresh fruit and a dusting of icing sugar, flavoured yoghurt or whipped cream.

ORANGE JULIA

This is our 'recreation' of a commercially made American drink enjoyed often in the past.

For 1 large or 2 small drinks:
4 ice cubes
1 cup orange juice
½ cup skim milk powder
½ tsp vanilla essence
1–2 tsp sugar or honey

Drop the ice cubes through the feed tube onto the rotating metal blades of a food processor. (The loud noise will only last a few seconds.) Before the chopped ice melts add the orange juice, skim milk powder, vanilla essence and

sugar or honey to taste and process until really frothy.

Serve immediately as 'breakfast in a glass' with a wide straw.

◀ *Pain Perdu*

Baking and Sweet Treats

This chapter contains a number of recipes which we think you will like, even if you do not bake on a regular basis, make desserts only occasionally, and strong-mindedly resist confections with coffee after dinner!

Muffins are the easiest thing to bake that we know of. Whether you choose sweet muffins to serve with tea or coffee, or make savoury muffins for a light lunch or snack, the enthusiasm with which they are received will probably encourage you to make more!

The same thing applies to home-made bread! Nobody can resist it, the smell through the house is wonderful, it is much cheaper than bought bread, and your friends are sure to be impressed with your efforts.

We feel that a cake is sometimes called for to celebrate a special occasion, so have given you four of our favourite recipes to choose from.

And, when you feel that dessert is called for, you may like to make our wonderful cheesecake, or produce an interesting strudel.

And, last but not least, our little 'goodies' finish off a special meal with style, and are nice to give to someone to say 'Thank you', or to mark a special anniversary.

Have fun with these recipes!

◀ **Dee's Festive Cheesecake**
Page 108

HERBED MINI MUFFINS

These very special little green-flecked muffins are everybody's favourites. Hot from the oven, they will disappear fast at any time of the day.

For about 12–18 mini muffins:
1 cup flour
2 tsp baking powder
1 cup (100g) grated tasty cheese
¼ cup chopped parsley
1 Tbsp chopped fresh herbs
1 spring onion, chopped
½ tsp salt
1 tsp sugar
⅛ tsp cayenne pepper
1 egg
½ cup + 2 Tbsp milk

Measure together into a large bowl the first nine ingredients. Use the fresh herbs you like best, or whichever will go well with the fillings or toppings you plan to use. (Use dill for salmon, basil for smoked meat.) Toss well to mix.

In another bowl, beat the egg and milk together with a fork or whisk. Tip the egg mixture into the dry ingredients and fold together, stirring just enough to dampen the flour. Do not overmix.

Spoon mixture into mini-muffin pans that have been evenly coated with non-stick spray.

Bake at 200°C for 10–12 minutes, until the centres spring back when pressed.

Serve whole or split from top to bottom, with savoury spreads, smoked salmon, shaved smoked meats, etc.

CHILLI CHEESE MUFFINS

Everybody loves these savoury muffins and they are easy to make. Save time and your knuckles by buying pregrated tasty cheese.

For 18 mini, 12 medium-sized or 6 monster muffins:
2 cups (200g) grated tasty cheese
1½ cups self-raising flour
½ tsp salt
¼ tsp chilli powder
1 Tbsp sugar
1 egg
1 cup milk

Measure the grated cheese, self-raising flour, salt, chilli powder, and sugar into a large bowl. Mix lightly with your fingertips to combine.

In a small container beat the egg and milk until evenly combined. Pour all the liquid onto the dry ingredients, then fold the two mixtures together, taking care not to overmix.

Spoon mixture into muffin pans that have been sprayed with non-stick spray. Sprinkle with a little extra cheese and chilli powder if you like.

Bake at 210°C for about 12 minutes, until muffins spring back when pressed in the middle and are golden brown.

Serve mini muffins for cocktail snacks or with morning coffee. Medium-sized or 'monster' muffins make good lunches.

SAM'S TOMATO MUFFINS

These tasty muffins are good all year round. They are quickly made with ingredients from your store cupboard.

For 12 medium-sized or 6 monster muffins:
425g can whole tomatoes
2 cups flour
4 tsp baking powder
½ tsp salt
½ cup grated cheese
50g butter, melted
1 egg
½ cup unsweetened yoghurt
½ cup tomato juice (reserved from can)
1 Tbsp pesto or 2 Tbsp chopped basil

Open and drain the tomatoes, reserving the juice. Cut tomatoes open and discard the seeds, then chop the flesh into small cubes, draining off any liquid.

Measure the flour, baking powder and salt into a bowl. Add the grated cheese and stir thoroughly.

In another bowl, whisk together the melted butter, egg, yoghurt, tomato juice and pesto. Stir this mixture and the drained, cubed tomatoes gently into the dry ingredients, taking care not to overmix.

Spoon the batter into muffin pans that have been sprayed with non-stick spray. Bake at 220°C for about 15 minutes, until lightly browned and the centres spring back when pressed.

Serve as a light meal with soup (pages 8–13) in winter, or with salad (pages 84–87) in summer.

HERBED PUMPKIN MUFFINS

Mashed pumpkin gives these muffins a wonderful colour. An interesting combination of herbs intensifies both the pumpkin and cheese flavours.

For 18 mini, 12 medium-sized or 6 monster muffins:

2 cups self-raising flour
¹/₂ tsp salt
1 Tbsp sugar
2 cups (200g) grated cheese
1¹/₂ tsp ground cumin
1 tsp oreganum
¹/₄–¹/₂ tsp cayenne pepper
1 egg
1 cup milk
1 cup (250g) mashed cooked pumpkin
1–2 Tbsp pumpkin seeds

Measure the first seven ingredients into a large bowl, crumbling the oreganum a little as you add it, and adding cayenne to suit your taste. Toss well, to mix all the dry ingredients thoroughly.

In a separate container mix the egg, milk and pumpkin. Beat together until well mixed.

Pour the liquid ingredients into the bowl containing the dry mixture. Without overmixing, fold everything together. The flour should be just dampened, not smooth.

Spray muffin pans with non-stick spray. Spoon the mixture into prepared muffin pans. Sprinkle a few pumpkin seeds over each one.

Bake at 220°C for 12–14 minutes, until golden brown and until centres spring back when pressed.

Serve warm as finger food for a party, or with soup for lunch.

101

▲ *Crunchy Lemon Muffins and Chocolate Banana Muffins*

CHOCOLATE BANANA MUFFINS

Here is a recipe that is well worth trying. The banana flavour is strongest when you use overripe bananas.

For 18 mini or 12 medium-sized muffins:

2 cups self-raising flour
$^1/_2$ cup caster sugar
$^1/_2$ cup chocolate chips
$^1/_2$ tsp salt
100g butter
1 cup milk
1 egg
1 tsp vanilla essence
1 cup (2 or 3) mashed bananas

With a fork, stir together in a large bowl the flour, caster sugar, chocolate chips and salt.

In another container, melt the butter, remove from the heat, then add the milk, egg and vanilla and beat well.

Mash and measure the bananas and stir them into the liquid mixture, mixing well to combine the ingredients. Tip into the bowl with the dry mixture. Fold everything together carefully until all the flour is dampened, stopping before the mixture is smooth.

Spray muffin pans with non-stick spray. Spoon the mixture into the prepared pans.

Bake at 220°C for 12–15 minutes, until muffins spring back when pressed in the centre.

Serve with tea or coffee at any time of the day. Mini muffins make good snacks for school lunch boxes.

CRUNCHY LEMON MUFFINS

A great favourite! The sugar and lemon juice drizzled over the top of these muffins after baking gives a tangy flavour and an interesting sugary crunch.

For 12 medium-sized muffins:
2 cups self-raising flour
¾ cup sugar
75g butter
1 cup milk
1 egg
grated rind of 1 large or 2 small lemons
¼ cup lemon juice
¼ cup sugar

Measure the flour and first measure of sugar into a bowl and toss to mix.

Melt the butter, add the milk, egg and lemon rind and beat well with a fork to combine.

Add the liquids to the dry ingredients and fold together until the dry ingredients have been lightly dampened but not thoroughly mixed.

Divide the mixture evenly between 12 medium-sized muffin pans that have been well coated with non-stick spray.

Bake at 200°C for 10 minutes.

Stir together the lemon juice and second measure of sugar without dissolving the sugar, and drizzle this over the hot muffins as soon as they are removed from the oven. Allow to stand in the pans only for a few minutes after this, in case the syrup hardens as it cools and sticks the muffins to their pans. If this happens, it may be necessary to use a knife to 'lever' the muffins from the pan. Take care not to damage the non-stick finish of the pans.

Serve with tea or coffee for afternoon tea, or as a dessert with lightly whipped cream and fresh fruit or berries.

FRUITED BRAN MUFFINS

Flavour these muffins with a different fruit each time you make them. We tried several variations, and each was delicious.

For about 15 medium-sized muffins:
¼ cup golden syrup
1 cup milk
½ cup raw sugar
¼ cup oil
2 eggs
1½ cups wheatbran
dried or fresh fruit*
1 cup plain or wholemeal flour
½ tsp baking soda
1½ tsp baking powder
1 tsp salt

*½ cup chopped dates or raisins or 2 ripe bananas, mashed, or 1 grated apple, or about 1 cup cubed fresh apricots, plums, peaches or nectarines

Soften the golden syrup by standing the can in hot water then measure the required amount into a large mixing bowl. Add milk, stir until the syrup dissolves then add the next four ingredients and beat well with a fork until well mixed.

Prepare the fruit of your choice and add to the golden syrup mixture. Sift the flour, baking soda, baking powder and salt into this and fold in gently until dry ingredients are dampened, taking care not to overmix.

Lightly spray the muffin pans with non-stick spray and divide the mixture evenly between the pans. Bake at 200°C for 15 minutes or until the centres will spring back when lightly pressed.

Serve warm, lightly spread with butter or cream cheese. Freeze extras until required.

FRUITY SPICED MUFFINS

These delicious spiced muffins can be cooked at Easter instead of Hot Cross Buns. They are sure to become family favourites!

For 30–36 mini-muffins or 15–18 medium-sized muffins:
2 cups self-raising flour
1–1½ cups good-quality dried mixed fruit
1 cup brown sugar
1 Tbsp mixed spice
1 Tbsp cinnamon
½ tsp ground cloves
1 large egg
1–1¼ cups milk
75g butter, melted

Measure the first six ingredients into a bowl, then mix well with your fingers. Use the larger quantity of mixed fruit for extra-fruity buns. (Use level measuring tablespoons of spices.)

Add egg and 1 cup of milk to the melted butter and beat with a fork. Stir all at once into dry mix, then fold together, without overmixing. If mixture is drier than a muffin batter, add extra milk.

Spray muffin pans with non-stick spray and spoon in mixture so each pan is three-quarters full.

Bake at 210°C for about 12 minutes, until centres spring back.

Serve warm, with tea or coffee for weekend brunch, and reheated at other times.

BREAD — SHAPE AND BAKE

*Using this basic recipe, then shaping it in different ways, you can make
a selection of interesting breads such as Quick Rolls, Pizza,
Pita Bread, Focaccia and Bread Sticks.*

2 tsp dry yeast granules
2 tsp sugar
1 cup warm water
1 Tbsp butter or oil
2–3 cups flour
1 tsp salt

Mix the yeast, sugar and lukewarm water together, add the butter or oil, cover and allow to stand in a warm place for 10 minutes or longer, until the yeast starts frothing. (The butter softens as it stands — it does not need to be melted.)

Warm the flour in a microwave oven for about 45 seconds on High (100% power), or in an oven that has been turned on for 5 minutes to 150°C then turned off. Stir enough warm flour into the bubbly yeast to make a dough firm enough to knead. Knead until smooth and satiny, about 5 minutes. (Do not add any more flour than you need.)

Turn the dough in a dribble of oil, in a microwavable bowl, cover the bowl, and leave to rise. The fastest way to rise it is to give it 1-minute bursts on Defrost (30% power) in the microwave oven, every 5–10 minutes or when the bowl of dough feels cold. The microwave is a good place to leave it to stand between bursts, too. Otherwise, use an oven, prewarmed as above, then turned off, or stand the covered bowl in a sink of lukewarm water that has been covered with a baking tray. When the dough is twice the size it was originally, sprinkle it with the salt, knead it again thoroughly, and shape it as you like. If it rises before you are ready for it, give it a short knead, cover it again, and leave it to stand at room temperature. Keep doing this as it rises again, until you are ready to shape it.

Round Rolls

Shape dough into about 16 round balls, dribble about a tablespoon of olive oil onto a sponge-roll sheet, and turn the rolls in this. Sprinkle them with grated parmesan or other cheese, or with toasted sesame seeds, or dried oreganum etc. Cover lightly with plastic cling film and leave in a warm place until they rise to almost twice their size. Bake at 220°C for 10–15 minutes, until browned, top and bottom.

Knotted Rolls

Cut dough into 12 pieces and roll each into a 25–26cm long 'pencil'. Knot each strip loosely, folding under ends to make a rosette if you like. Put the shaped rolls on a lightly oiled oven tray. Cover lightly with plastic cling film and leave in a warm place until they rise to almost twice their size. Brush very gently with beaten egg then sprinkle with poppy seeds, toasted sesame seeds or finely grated cheese. Bake at 220°C for 10–15 minutes, until golden brown.

Bread Sticks

Roll dough into about 20 long thin sticks, each about 20cm long. Place on an oiled oven tray, brush with lightly beaten egg white, then sprinkle liberally with parmesan cheese, toasted sesame seeds or poppy seeds. Allow to stand for 10 minutes, then bake at 180°C for about 20 minutes, until dried through and lightly browned. Store in airtight containers.

Pizza

Press or roll dough out to form a large circle, eight small circles, or to fill a large sponge-roll tin. Use grainy corn meal to stop shaped pizzas sticking to the oven tray etc. Top with your favourite pizza toppings and bake at 220–230°C until the cheese melts and the base is browned slightly, from 5–15 minutes, depending on size and thickness.

Pita Bread

Cut dough into eight equal parts, roll each out into a 15–18cm circle on a well-floured or cornmealed working surface, then allow to stand for about 10 minutes. Have oven heated to its highest temperature, with an oven tray, cast iron pan or griddle heated in the middle of it. Slide the first-rolled circle onto a piece of cardboard etc., then open the oven door briefly and transfer it quickly onto the heated oven tray. In 1–2 minutes the bread should rise into a ball, then deflate. Lift out with tongs after 2–3 minutes, and put the next pita bread in to cook. Pile the cooked pita breads in a plastic bag so they do not dry out.

Bread base for Melts

Divide the dough into two equal parts, roll each into a ball. Place on a lightly oiled oven tray and roll out until about 1cm thick. Cover with plastic cling film and leave to rise in a warm place until they have doubled in size. Bake at 220°C for about 10 to 15 minutes.

(See recipe for Melts page 74.)

Focaccia

Press the dough into one large or two small olive-oiled sponge-roll tins, leaving finger-hole depressions. Top with chopped olives, sautéed onion rings, sage or rosemary, sun-dried tomatoes, etc., then dribble 2–3 tablespoons of olive oil over the top. Leave to rise in a warm place for about 15 minutes, then bake at 220°C until golden brown, about 10–15 minutes. Serve warm, in rectangles.

Pan Bread

Melt 2 tablespoons of butter in an electric frypan, then turn the pan off, it should be warm, not hot to rise the bread.

Roll dough into 16 or 25 even sized balls then turn in the melted butter in the frypan. Arrange rolls so they all fit, and flatten each one slightly. Put the lid on the pan and leave the rolls to rise for about 15 minutes.

When dough has risen to almost double its original size, turn the pan on to 150°C. Keep the lid on and the steam vent closed. After about 5 minutes the rolls should have risen more, be fairly firm and dry (and white) on the top, and be golden brown on the bottom. Turn over, one at a time, or in one piece. Cook for 3–5 minutes longer with the steam vent open, so the tops of the rolls are still warm, but some steam can escape.

Pan Bread, Focaccia and Knotted Rolls ▶

▲ *Lemon Yoghurt Cake*

LEMON YOGHURT CAKE

*Because this cake contains oil, it is very easy to mix, either in a food processor, or
in a bowl, using a rotary beater, whisk or fork.*

1¾ cups sugar
rind of 2 lemons
2 eggs
1 cup oil
½ tsp salt
1 cup yoghurt
2–3 Tbsp lemon juice
2 cups self-raising flour

If you are using a food processor, put the sugar into the (dry) bowl with the metal chopping blade. Peel all the yellow peel from the lemons, using a potato peeler, and add to the bowl. Run the machine until the lemon peel is finely chopped through the sugar.

Add the eggs, oil and salt and process until thick and smooth, then add the yoghurt and lemon juice and blend enough to mix. Use any kind of yoghurt — plain, sweetened or flavoured. (If you use flavoured yoghurt, choose a flavour that will blend with the colour and flavour of the lemon.)

Add the flour and process just enough

to combine with the rest of the mixture.

If you are mixing in a bowl, grate all the coloured peel from the lemons, and beat it with the oil, eggs and sugar before adding the remaining ingredients, in the same order as above.

Pour cake mixture into a buttered and floured ring pan. Bake at 180°C for 30 minutes, or until the sides start to shrink, the centre springs back when pressed, and a skewer comes out clean. Leave to cool for about 10 minutes before turning carefully out onto a rack.

Serve sprinkled with a little icing sugar, with whipped cream if you like.

JANE'S BANANA CAKE

The flavour of this cake depends on the ripeness of the bananas. Make it with overripe bananas if possible.

1½ cups self-raising flour
1 tsp baking soda
3 ripe bananas
125g butter, at room temperature
¾ cup sugar
2 eggs
2 Tbsp milk
1 tsp vanilla essence

Sift the flour and baking soda together into a large bowl.

Mash the bananas roughly with a fork. Put them in a food processor with the remaining ingredients and process until smooth. Add to the flour and mix until just combined.

Pour into a 20cm ring pan that has been lined with baking paper or a non-stick Teflon liner.

Bake at 180°C for 35–40 minutes, or until a skewer comes out clean.

Serve dusted with icing sugar, or topped with your favourite icing if you like. The chocolate icing from Kirsten's Chocolate Cake (below) is suitable.

PINEAPPLE CARROT CAKE

The flavour of this cake is truly delicious. You can identify the different ingredients in every mouthful.

2 cups self-raising flour
½ tsp baking soda
1 cup sugar
¾ cup coconut
½ cup chopped walnuts
1 tsp salt
2 tsp cinnamon
2 cups grated carrot
3 eggs
1 cup oil
1 tsp vanilla
225g can crushed pineapple

Sift the flour into a large bowl, add baking soda, sugar, coconut, walnuts, salt, cinnamon and the grated carrot. Toss with a fork to mix well.

In another bowl, beat the eggs, oil, vanilla and pineapple, using a fork. Stir this mixture into the dry ingredients, mixing until just combined. (This mixture is firmer than many carrot cakes.)

Pour the mixture into a 23cm square baking pan lined with baking paper or a non-stick Teflon liner.

Bake at 160°C for 45–50 minutes, or until the centre of the cake springs back when pressed.

Serve with yoghurt or lightly whipped cream, with coffee or for dessert, or top with a lemon, orange, or cream cheese icing.

KIRSTEN'S CHOCOLATE CAKE

This chocolate cake always arouses comment, because of its moistness, soft texture, and flavour.

125g butter
2 rounded household Tbsp golden syrup
2 eggs
2 cups flour
2 Tbsp cocoa
2 tsp baking powder
2 tsp baking soda
1 cup sugar
1½ cups milk

Heat the butter until melted, then stir in the golden syrup. Stir to combine the two, warming again only if necessary. Put everything else in the food processor, with the eggs first, and the milk last. Mix in brief bursts, then add the golden syrup and butter mixture, and process for two 30-second bursts, scraping down the sides of the food processor after the first burst.

Bake in two 20cm round pans if you want to fill it with fresh or mock cream or intend to make a layer cake (with four layers of cake). For a rectangular, unfilled cake, bake in a rectangular pan about 22 x 27cm with rounded corners. (Line bottom and sides of square or rectangular pans with baking paper. Line the bottom of round tins and

spray or butter their sides.)

Bake at 180°C for 25 minutes, or until the centre springs back when pressed, and a skewer in the centre comes out clean.

Ice with chocolate icing.

Chocolate Icing:
1 Tbsp butter
2 Tbsp hot water
1 Tbsp cocoa
1 cup icing sugar
Heat butter, water and cocoa together until the butter has melted and all ingredients are easily combined. Add sifted icing sugar and mix thoroughly until icing is smooth.

Serve within three days. The texture is best the day it is made.

DEE'S FESTIVE CHEESECAKE

(See photograph pages 98–99.)
Dee's smooth and creamy cheesecake is the best that we have ever made — or tasted. It is very rich, so it should be served only as an occasional treat.

For 8–12 servings:
1 packet (250g) digestive biscuits
100g butter
750g (3 cartons) cream cheese
1 cup sugar
2 large eggs
1 tsp vanilla essence

Crumb the biscuits, using a food processor if available, or put them into a plastic bag and crush with a rolling pin.

Melt the butter and add the biscuit crumbs. Mix well and press onto the bottom and sides of a 20 or 23cm springform or loose-bottomed cake tin.

Beat the cream cheese and sugar until soft and fluffy. Add eggs one at a time, then add the vanilla. Pour the mixture into the prepared biscuit base.

Bake at 160°C for 40–50 minutes, until centre is firm, taking care not to brown the top too much. Leave in the oven to cool.

Refrigerate until ready to serve.

To serve, pile fresh berries on top. Sprinkle these with icing sugar. Spoon lightly whipped cream onto wedges.

FILO APPLE STRUDEL

When this dessert is made with filo pastry, it is much lighter and crisper than traditional strudel.

For 6 servings:
¼ cup blanched almonds
1 slice (toast thickness) bread
3 apples
½ cup sultanas
¼ cup sugar
1 tsp cinnamon
½ cup sour cream
1 egg yolk, lightly beaten
9 sheets filo pastry
oil or butter for brushing

Chop the blanched almonds roughly in a food processor bowl. Add the bread and process until crumbed. Cut unpeeled apples in quarters, remove the cores, cut apples in rough slices and add to the bowl. Process in bursts until apples are chopped to the size of peas.

Add the next five ingredients and mix until just combined.

Take three sheets of filo pastry and, working quickly on a dry bench, lie them side by side, long sides together with the edges slightly overlapping. Brush each sheet lightly with oil or butter. (Use no more than a teaspoon per sheet, as the whole surface need not be covered.) Cover with three more sheets, oil or butter in the same way, then top with the remaining three sheets. You will end up with a large rectangle, three layers thick.

Place the prepared filling along the short edge of the large rectangle, then roll up loosely. Cover the ends of the roll with tinfoil, so the filling will not fall out during cooking.

Place on an oven tray and bake at 180°C for 15–20 minutes, until golden brown.

Note:
If you have a small processor, you may have to process the filling in two batches. (Filling may also be mixed after chopping nuts and apples by hand.)

Serve soon after cooking, hot or warm, with whipped cream.

FRESH FRUIT BUCKLE

This dessert is nice even if you only have a handful of raw cubed fruit or berries to scatter over its surface. Great fun made with the first blackberries picked from the side of the road.

For 6–9 servings:
50g butter
½ cup brown sugar
1 egg
1 cup flour
1½ tsp baking powder
½ tsp cinnamon
¼ cup milk
1–3 cups berries or fresh fruit, cubed*

Topping:
½ cup flour
¼ cup brown sugar
½ tsp cinnamon
50g cold butter

*cubed raw peaches, nectarines, kiwifruit, strawberries, or whole blueberries, raspberries, black currants, grapes

Melt the butter until barely liquid. Add the sugar and egg and beat until creamy. Sift in the dry ingredients, then tip in the milk, and fold all together until blended, without overmixing. Spread thinly over a buttered, sprayed or lined 23cm square cake tin.

Sprinkle the cleaned berries or cubed fruit evenly over the surface.

To make the topping, using a food processor or pastry blender, cut or rub the topping ingredients together to make a crumbly mixture. Sprinkle this over the fruit layer, covering the complete surface as evenly as possible.

Bake at 180°C for 45–60 minutes or until firm in the middle.

Serve warm or reheated, dusted with icing sugar and with lightly whipped cream or ice cream.

MEXICAN FLANS

These moulded caramel custards are a lower-fat variation of an old favourite.
They are quite easy to make in bulk if you use deep muffin pans.

For 12 unmoulded custards:
½ cup sugar
4 eggs
½ of a 400g can sweetened condensed
   milk
1 litre milk
½–1 tsp vanilla essence

Spray a tray of deep non-stick muffin pans with non-stick spray.

Put the sugar in a small, preferably non-stick frypan and heat gently, shaking the pan to move the sugar around. Do not stir it. If the sugar starts to brown unevenly, lower the heat. (Dark brown caramel is bitter.)

Pour the caramel into the prepared muffin pans, tilting to coat bottoms evenly.

Beat together the eggs, condensed milk, milk and vanilla. Pour through a fine sieve into a jug, then pour into the muffin pans. Stand the tray in a roasting dish of hot water.

Bake uncovered at 150°C, for about 15 minutes or until the centres feel firm and a sharp knife inserted in the middle of a custard comes out clean.

Cool to room temperature, then chill for at least 4 hours. Unmould carefully, pushing one side of pudding down with your fingers until the pudding flips over and sits caramel-side up, on your cupped fingers. Use a sharp knife if the custards stick to the sides. Slip on to individual dishes.

Serve with caramel liquid poured over each custard. Garnish with a fanned strawberry and a spoonful of lightly whipped cream if you like.

EASY CHOCOLATE FUDGE

Chocolate fudge is always a great favourite. This version is exceptionally quick and easy and requires no beating.

Makes 64 squares:
500g dark chocolate
400g can sweetened condensed milk
½ tsp vanilla essence
walnut halves to decorate (optional)

Break up the chocolate if necessary. Heat the condensed milk with the broken chocolate in a heavy pot, over a low heat, or in a microwave oven on Medium (50% power), stirring frequently until the chocolate is melted and the two are well blended.

Add the vanilla, stir well and pour into 20cm cake tin that has been lined with baking paper or a Teflon liner.

Leave until firm, then cut into eight strips. Cut each strip into eight squares and top each with a walnut half if you like. Cover and store in a cool place for up to a week.

Gift-pack by lining an attractive box or small basket and filling it with fudge.

FABULOUS FUDGE

This delicious soft, smooth fudge is made in a microwave oven.
It will melt in your mouth.

Makes 64 squares:
100g butter
1 cup sugar
¼ cup golden syrup
400g can sweetened condensed milk
1 tsp vanilla essence

Mix all ingredients except vanilla in a flat-bottomed casserole, or a microwave jug resistant to high heat.

Microwave on High (100% power) for 11–12 minutes, stirring every 2 minutes. At the end point all sugar should have dissolved, the mixture should have bubbled vigorously all over the surface, and formed a soft ball in cold water.

Add vanilla. Don't worry if the mixture

looks slightly curdled or buttery. Beat with a wooden spoon for about 5 minutes, or until mixture loses its gloss. Spoon the mixture into a lightly buttered or sprayed 20cm cake tin. Let stand for about an hour, then cut into eight strips. Cut each strip into eight squares.

Serve as an after-dinner treat or use as a gift.

LIQUEUR TRUFFLES

These truffles are the ultimate in luxury, and are very rich.
Definitely not for the children!

Makes about 24 truffles:
150g dark cooking chocolate
2 Tbsp orange-flavoured liqueur
2 Tbsp butter
1 egg yolk
¼ cup cocoa

Break the chocolate up if necessary. Put into a microwavable dish with your chosen liqueur. Heat for 3–4 minutes on Defrost (30% power) until the chocolate is soft and will combine easily with the liqueur.

Add the butter and egg yolk and mix until well combined (the warm

chocolate will melt the butter). Leave aside for 3–4 hours at room temperature before rolling into walnut-sized balls. Roll each ball in cocoa.

Serve on very special occasions, as an after-dinner treat.

CHOCOLATE TRUFFLES

Use crumbs from a plain chocolate cake to make these little truffles. Light cake crumbs will do at a pinch, but the colour of the finished truffles is not so rich and dark.

For about 48 truffles:
1 cup currants
2 Tbsp finely grated orange rind
¼ cup rum, whisky, brandy or orange juice
125g dark or cooking chocolate
250g (2½ cups) chocolate cake crumbs
¼ cup coarse desiccated coconut

Put the currants in a sieve and pour boiling water through them, drain and then put into a bowl with the grated orange rind, the spirit of your choice or the same amount of juice from the orange.

Break up and melt the chocolate, heating it until it is liquid, either in a microwave oven for about 4 minutes on Medium (50% power), or over a pot of

hot but not boiling water. Add the melted chocolate and the cake crumbs to the currant mixture, and mix well.

Divide mixture into four parts, then each part into 12. Roll into balls, then roll each ball in coconut. Refrigerate or freeze until ready to use.

Serve with after-dinner coffee, or package attractively for a gift from your kitchen.

◄ *From top to bottom: Easy Chocolate Fudge, Liqueur Truffles, Fabulous Fudge, Chocolate Truffles*

REFERENCE RECIPES

Croutons

Croutons make a wonderful addition to many salads. They add interesting textures to creamed soups, too.

2 Tbsp olive or other oil
1 clove garlic, sliced
2 (toast thickness) slices white bread

In a frypan over low heat, warm the olive oil with the garlic. Remove garlic before it browns.

Cut the bread into small cubes, toss in the garlic oil, then cook on medium heat, turning frequently, until croutons are golden brown, about 20 minutes.

If preferred, brown under a grill, checking regularly to prevent uneven browning. Or bake at 150°C for about 5 minutes or until golden brown.

Crostini

Make these ahead and store in an airtight container to have on hand when guests arrive.

1 loaf french bread
flavourings*
¼ cup olive oil
* parmesan cheese, pesto, tapenade,
*   mixed mustard, ground cumin,*
*   Tabasco sauce, etc.*

Slice the loaf of bread diagonally into 1cm slices. Mix the flavourings of your choice with the olive oil in a shallow bowl and brush or spread evenly over the sliced bread.

Arrange on a baking tray that has been lightly sprayed or lined with a non-stick liner and bake at 150°C for 5–10 minutes till golden brown and crisp. When cold store in airtight containers for up to a week until needed.

Serve with soup, dips, pâtés or nibbles with drinks.

Melba Toast

Cut stale bread rolls or french bread into very thin slices, using a sharp serrated knife. Bake at 150–180°C in one layer on an oven tray until the bread browns very slightly. Cooking time will vary with the type of bread, its thickness and its staleness. Start to check after 3–4 minutes.

When cold, store in airtight jars or plastic bags. Refresh for 10 minutes at 150°C before serving, if you like.

Garlic Bread

Make ahead, and cook or reheat when needed.

1 loaf french bread
50g butter
2 cloves garlic, finely chopped
2–4 Tbsp finely chopped parsley or other fresh herbs

Cut the loaf into diagonal 1cm slices, without cutting through the bottom crust, so the loaf holds together.

Soften, but do not melt the butter, then add the chopped garlic and herbs and mix to combine.

Spread the flavoured butter on the cut slices of the bread, wrap the loaf in foil, leaving the top exposed, and bake at 200°C for about 10 minutes, or at a lower temperature for longer, until the top crust is crisp and the loaf has heated right through.

Vegetable Stock

Well-flavoured vegetable stock may be made in 30 minutes if you start with very finely chopped vegetables.

For 3–4 cups:
1 large onion
3 cloves garlic
1 large carrot
1–2 stalks celery
1 Tbsp tomato paste
1 sprig parsley
1 sprig oreganum
1 tsp crushed black peppercorns
1 dried chilli
1 bay leaf
4 cups water
1 tsp sugar
about 1 tsp salt

Quarter but do not peel the onion. Put in a food processor bowl with the unpeeled garlic cloves, the scrubbed but unpeeled carrot cut in chunks, the broken stalks of celery with their leaves removed, the tomato paste, parsley and oreganum. Process finely using the metal chopping blade.

Transfer the chopped vegetables to a large pot, add crushed peppercorns, chilli, bay leaf and water. Simmer for 20 minutes then press through a sieve, extracting as much liquid as possible. Add the sugar and salt to taste. Freeze for up to 6 months.

Chicken Stock

Although you can simmer chicken bones, giblets (available from larger supermarkets) give a stronger-flavoured stock with minimum cost and effort.

500g chicken giblets
1–2 cloves garlic
1–2 slices fresh ginger (optional)
1 Tbsp light soya sauce
1 Tbsp sherry
freshly ground black pepper
8 cups (2 litres) water

Put all the ingredients in a large pot and simmer for 2–3 hours. Strain, reserving the cooked giblets if you like. They can be chopped and added to the soup before serving.

Use the stock immediately, store in the refrigerator for up to three days or freeze in covered containers for up to six months.

Fish Stock

Fish stock requires only a short cooking time. When you make it, open the window so the odours are quickly dispersed.

For 3–4 cups:
about 750g fish skeletons and/or fish heads
1 onion, sliced
1–2 garlic cloves
1 stalk celery, chopped
1 bay leaf
1 sprig parsley
1 sprig thyme
6 peppercorns or 1 dried chilli
2–3 cm strip lemon rind
4 cups water

Put all the ingredients listed in a fairly large pot. Cover and simmer for 30 minutes, then strain through a sieve and wrap and discard the debris. Strain the stock through muslin again, if it is to be used in a light-coloured sauce or soup where no specks are wanted.

Refrigerate or freeze in 1-cup portions, up to 6 months.

Note:
Fresh salmon trimmings make excellent stock if they are available.

Pesto

Fresh basil has a wonderful flavour but a short season. Making pesto is a way of enjoying it all year.

1½–2 cups lightly packed basil leaves
½ cup parsley
2 cloves garlic
2–4 Tbsp parmesan cheese
2 Tbsp pinenuts, almonds or walnuts
¼–½ cup olive oil
about ½ tsp salt

Wash the basil to minimise later browning, then drain on a cloth or paper towel. Remove the tough stems and put the basil, parsley and peeled garlic cloves into a food processor with the parmesan cheese and nuts. Process, adding up to ¼ cup of oil, until finely chopped. Keep adding oil until you have a dark green paste, just liquid enough to pour. Add salt to taste.

Store pesto in the refrigerator in a lidded container for up to three months, or freeze for longer storage.

Note:
Pesto may darken at top of jars where it is exposed to air. Make sure there is a layer of oil at the top of each jar.

Quick Tapenade

This mixture has a very strong, concentrated flavour. Its colour varies with the darkness of the olives used.

1 cup sliced black olives
2–4 cloves garlic, peeled
2 or 3 anchovy fillets (omit for a
*   vegetarian version)*
1 Tbsp capers
1 Tbsp caper liquid
1 Tbsp lemon or lime juice
2–3 Tbsp olive oil

Finely chop (but do not purée) all ingredients, except the olive oil, using a food processor.

Add 2 tablespoons of the oil to the mixture and spoon into a jar, pour the remaining oil over the top, and close with a screw-on airtight seal.

Use as a spread, toss through pasta with additional olive oil or pesto, or add to dressings and dips.

Store in the refrigerator for up to a month.

Sun-Dried Tomato Paste

This mixture is dark red in colour and is strongly flavoured. It makes a delicious spread for crackers, french bread, etc., and adds colour and flavour to dressings, dips, spreads and sauces.

sun-dried tomatoes (equivalent of 3
*   tomatoes)*
2 Tbsp wine, sherry or balsamic vinegar
¼ small red onion, chopped
3–4 Tbsp olive oil, or oil from tomatoes
½–1 roasted, peeled red pepper
*   (optional)*
salt and pepper
sugar
fresh or dried chilli

Chop the (drained) sun-dried tomatoes in a food processor or blender with the best quality vinegar you have, then add the other ingredients.

If you have sun-dried tomatoes packed in oil, use some of this to make the paste, otherwise, use olive oil.

Allow to stand in the food processor/ blender for about 15 minutes then add more vinegar or oil to thin it to a thin paste, and process again. Taste and season as you like, using some or all of the suggested flavourings.

Store in a covered container in the fridge for up to two weeks.

Roasting Peppers

To roast whole or halved peppers, place under the grill and grill until blackened and swollen, turning several times to roast evenly. Or cook in a roasting dish at 220°C for 30–40 minutes until the skin and edges blacken and the flesh softens.

Remove the peppers from the oven and allow to stand in a plastic oven bag for about 5 minutes. Remove from the bag and peel off the skin, while holding under cold water.

Savoury Kibbled Wheat

Precooking in oil gives this chopped wheat a lovely nutty flavour.

1 onion, finely chopped
2 cloves garlic, finely chopped
2 Tbsp oil
1 cup kibbled wheat
2 cups water
1 tsp instant stock powder
¼ cup fresh herbs, finely chopped

Cook the onion and garlic in the oil until lightly browned. Add the kibbled wheat and cook over a moderate heat for 2–3 minutes. Add the water and instant stock powder, cover and simmer gently for 20–30 minutes or until the water has been absorbed and the grain is tender.

Stir in the chopped fresh herbs 5 minutes before serving.

Liptauer Cheese

Our version of this tasty Austrian spread is wonderful sprinkled with chopped chives, on crackers, Melba Toast or Crostini (page 112).

1 cup (250g) cottage cheese
100g butter, softened
1 tsp paprika
1 tsp ground caraway seeds
2 tsp chopped capers
1–2 tsp chopped anchovies
1 tsp mixed mustard
2 Tbsp chopped chives

Beat all the ingredients together, until light, well mixed and creamy, using a food processor or a bowl and a wooden spoon.

Refrigerate in a covered container until required. It tastes best when eaten within 24 hours, but can be kept for up to a month.

Note:
Grind the caraway seeds with a pestle and mortar (or hammer) just before using them.

Mexican Coating Mixture

If you like the flavour of the herbs and spices used in Mexican cooking, mix them in a screw-topped jar so you have them on hand. Use to flavour chicken for a quickly prepared meal.

For about ⅓ cup:
1 Tbsp paprika
1 Tbsp oreganum
1 Tbsp ground cumin
1 Tbsp onion or garlic salt
1 Tbsp flour
2 tsp caster sugar
about 1 tsp chilli powder

Mix all the ingredients, crumbling leaves of oreganum, if you like. Use less chilli powder for less hotness.

Store in an airtight container.

Tomato Salsa

This delicious fat-free sauce, dip or spread adds flavour to many bland foods.

¼ red onion
1 clove garlic
2 spring onions, chopped
2 pickled jalapeno peppers or ¼–½ tsp
  chilli powder
¼ cup roughly chopped coriander
4 large ripe tomatoes (blanched) or 400g
  can whole tomatoes, drained
1 Tbsp tomato paste
3 Tbsp wine vinegar
1 tsp oreganum
1 tsp salt

Put the first three ingredients in a food processor and process until coarsely chopped. Add peppers and coriander, process briefly, then add remaining ingredients and chop just enough to roughly cut the tomatoes. Take care not to over-process — the mixture should be red flecked with green.

For best flavour, stand for at least an hour before serving. Store covered in the refrigerator for up to two weeks.

Curry Powder and Paste

Double the amount of chilli powder in this recipe if you want a fiery mixture. It is interesting and mildly hot the way it is. When you make your own curry mixtures you roast the whole seeds before grinding them. This gives an aromatic mixture that will make tasty curries for six months or so!

To make about 100g:
2 Tbsp coriander seeds
1½ Tbsp cumin seeds
5cm piece cassia or cinnamon stick
1 tsp fennel seeds
1 tsp black mustard seeds
1 tsp cardamom seeds
½ tsp celery seeds
3 or 4 whole cloves
2 or 3 bay leaves

Ground spices:
2 tsp turmeric
2 tsp garlic powder
1 tsp powdered ginger
¼–½ tsp chilli powder

In a dry frypan or under a preheated grill, heat the whole spices, stirring at intervals, until they smell aromatic and you see them lightly smoking. Cool and grind finely, mix with the ground spices, and store in an airtight container in a cool place, away from the light, or use to make curry paste as follows:

Place the curry powder in a bowl. Mix with ½ cup of mild vinegar and allow to stand for at least 10 minutes.

Heat ½ cup of oil in a frypan or wok and add the paste to the oil (it will splatter so take care). Heat, stirring all the time to prevent sticking, until the water has boiled away (about 5 minutes). At this stage the paste will make a regular bubbling noise when you don't stir it. Take off the heat and allow to stand for 3–4 minutes. If the oil floats to the top, the spices are cooked. If not, add a little more oil and carry on cooking and stirring.

Bottle in sterilised jars and top the paste with a little more heated oil. Seal jars and store in a cool place.

Garam Masala

This spice mixture is usually added to curries close to the end of their cooking time.

¼ cup coriander seeds
2 Tbsp cumin seeds
1 Tbsp aniseed
2cm piece cassia or cinnamon stick
1 Tbsp cardamom seeds
1½ tsp cloves
½ tsp dried mint
2 bay leaves
pinch of saffron (optional)

Lightly roast all ingredients under a low-to-medium grill, until you see them smoking lightly and they smell aromatic. Cool and grind finely, in batches if necessary.

After grinding, mix thoroughly and store in an airtight jar in a cool place away from the light. Use within six months for maximum flavour.

Don't worry if you cannot find every ingredient. You can leave one or two out and still produce mixtures that taste very good. When you roast, grind and cook the spice mixtures, wear old clothes. They are likely to smell strongly of spices for some time!

Mild Curry Sauce

This type of mild curry sauce can be used as the basis for many Indian-style dishes, with additional spices and flavourings added along the way.

For 3–4 servings:
2 tsp curry powder
1 tsp paprika
1 tsp turmeric
2 Tbsp water
2 Tbsp oil
2 or 3 cloves garlic, finely chopped
1–2cm fresh ginger, grated
1 medium-sized onion, finely chopped
1 Tbsp tomato paste
1 cup water

Make a paste with the spices and water, then allow to stand for at least 5 minutes.

Heat the oil in a frypan or pot. Add the garlic and cook for 1 minute, then add the ginger and spice paste and cook for 30 seconds, stirring constantly.

Add the onion and stir-fry for about 10 minutes, before adding the tomato paste mixed with the water. Bring to the boil, turn the heat down and simmer gently for 10 minutes, stirring occasionally.

114

REFERENCE RECIPES

Sweet and Sour Sauce

Serve this sauce over egg-crumbed fish fingers or meatballs on rice.

2 Tbsp cornflour
½ cup sugar
1 Tbsp light soya sauce
1 Tbsp olive or other oil
¼ cup wine vinegar
¾ cup water
red food colouring (optional)

Mix the cornflour and sugar thoroughly, then add the remaining ingredients. Bring to the boil, stirring constantly, then thin with more hot water if desired.

Maharajah's Chutney

This mixture is delicious, unusual and very popular with our family and friends.

10 plump cloves garlic, chopped
500g onions, chopped
2 tsp grated fresh ginger
1 Tbsp black mustard seeds
5 small dried chillies
3 Tbsp coriander seeds
2 Tbsp cumin seeds, crushed
1 Tbsp cinnamon
2 tsp turmeric
½ cup oil
2 Tbsp salt
2 cups each malt vinegar and sugar
500g sultanas, roughly chopped
2 lemons, grated rind and juice

Mix the garlic, onions, and ginger in a bowl.

Using a pestle and mortar, a coffee and spice grinder or a heavy-duty plastic bag and a hammer, break up the next four ingredients together. Heat them in a large, heavy-based pot until fragrant, then add the cinnamon and turmeric, and heat through. Add about 2 tablespoons of oil, then the onion mixture, and cook for about 5 minutes.

Measure and add remaining ingredients, including the rest of the oil. Bring to the boil and simmer for about 1 hour, stirring frequently.

Pour hot chutney into clean heated jars, and top immediately with boiled screw-on metal lids.

Mayonnaise

Quick and easy to make in the food processor, this sauce is delicious and versatile. It puts most bought mayonnaise to shame!

1 egg
½ tsp salt
½ tsp sugar
1 tsp Dijon mustard
2 Tbsp wine vinegar
about 1 cup olive or other oil

Measure the first five ingredients into a food processor or blender. Turn on and add the oil in a thin stream until the mayonnaise is as thick and creamy as you like it. Keep in a covered container in the refrigerator for up to three weeks.

Tartare Sauce

This is particularly good with plainly cooked fish, but may be used in many other situations too.

2 or 3 spring onions, chopped
1 or 2 gherkins
1 Tbsp capers, chopped
1 tsp chopped parsley
lemon juice (optional)
1 cup mayonnaise

Prepare the first five ingredients, then stir into the mayonnaise. Allow to stand for at least an hour before serving to allow the flavour to develop. Thin with lemon juice if desired.

Hollandaise Sauce

Rich and delicious — a special-occasion sauce to dress up plainly cooked food.

For about 4 servings:
2 egg yolks
2–3 Tbsp lemon juice
100g butter

Break egg yolks into the bowl of a food processor fitted with a metal chopping blade. Add the lemon juice and process to combine.

Cut the butter into cubes and melt in the microwave oven in a microwavable jug, covered with a plate to avoid splattering. Heat on High (100% power) for 2–3 minutes until very hot and bubbling vigorously.

With the processor on, add the bubbling hot butter in a thin stream onto egg yolks. If sauce is not thick, heat gently in the microwave for 1 minute on Defrost (30% power), stirring after 30 seconds.

If making ahead, reheat by standing in a bowl of bath-temperature water, stirring occasionally. Sauce curdles if overheated.

Serve warm.

Peanut Sauce

This unusual sauce is delicious with chicken or vegetarian dishes. It can also be served as a dip, with crisp fresh vegetables.

2 garlic cloves, chopped
2 tsp grated fresh ginger
1 tsp freshly ground coriander seeds
*   (optional)*
2 Tbsp dark soya sauce
2 tsp lemon juice
1 Tbsp oil
3–4 drops Tabasco Sauce
¼ cup brown sugar
2 Tbsp peanut butter
¼ cup water

Combine all ingredients and heat until smooth and thickened. Dilute with water if too thick.

Satay Sauce

Brush small amounts of this sauce over chicken pieces before cooking, or serve over plain cooked vegetables.

½ cup chopped roasted peanuts
4 pieces crystallised ginger
1 Tbsp brown sugar
½ tsp ground coriander
2 cloves garlic, chopped
juice of 1 lemon
2 Tbsp light soya sauce
3–4 drops Tabasco sauce
1 Tbsp oil
1 cup coconut milk

Using a food processor or blender, chop the first 5 ingredients together until very fine, then add the next 4 ingredients and process again.

Gradually add the coconut milk until the sauce is the consistency of thin gravy.

Heat until it boils and thickens.

Serve hot or cold.

ABOUT INGREDIENTS

You will be able to make many of the recipes in this book using ingredients already in your store cupboard and refrigerator (or readily available at your local supermarket).

Some of the Asian recipes may contain ingredients with which you are not familiar, and do not have on hand initially. So that you can make these recipes too, we suggest you go to a large supermarket, or a store specialising in Asian supplies, and buy the following ingredients.

Kaffir lime leaves
Thai fish sauce
Green curry paste
Red curry paste
Dark sesame oil
Star anise
(Indian) curry paste

These will keep for months (if not longer) and will mean you can widen your day-to-day repertoire.

Anchovies

These are canned or bottled salty fillets of fish, which give a strong (but not fishy) flavour to foods. Once a container is opened you can refrigerate the contents in their oil for several months, or eat leftovers as they are on buttered french bread — wonderful!

Breads

Many foods may be served with bread. Look around — there are many exciting types to enjoy. If you have to buy more than you need, freeze the extra as soon as possible. Toast, microwave or barbecue to freshen.

Coriander

Fresh coriander leaves have a strong, distinctive flavour and may be grown in a warm place in your garden, bought in packets in large supermarkets, or in larger bunches, more cheaply, in stores that specialise in Asian foods. John West minced coriander leaf from most supermarkets is an acceptable substitute for freshly chopped leaves. It will keep in your refrigerator for some weeks. Use the same quantity (1 teaspoon paste for

1 teaspoon chopped fresh leaf). Other names for coriander include cilantro and Chinese parsley. Coriander seed (or ground coriander) has quite a different flavour, and should not be used in the place of coriander leaf.

Fish Sauce

Thai fish sauce is salty like soya sauce but has a unique flavour of its own. If you like Thai food, a bottle of this is worth having on hand. Like soya sauce it keeps indefinitely. Thai fish sauce can be found in some supermarkets or Asian food stores. If necessary, replace with light soya sauce.

Fresh Basil and Basil Pesto

There is no real substitute for fresh basil, but homemade or good bought basil pesto is the next best thing. Use about 1 Tbsp pesto in place of 2 Tbsp chopped fresh basil. Pesto in a recipe can be replaced with fresh basil in the proportions given above. If you have only dried basil on hand, use 1 tsp in place of 1 Tbsp pesto or 2 Tbsp fresh basil. It is better than nothing!

Garlic

We usually use fresh garlic, but you can use garlic paste/purée in its place. Use ½ teaspoon paste/purée in the place of one fresh clove.

To remove the skin from garlic, cut the root end off and flatten the clove with the bottom of a glass bottle or jar. If you use the right amount of force you should be able to simply lift away the skin.

Ginger

Fresh root ginger has a much more aromatic flavour than ground or crystallised ginger. Fresh root ginger will keep for several weeks in the fridge, and freezes well (it may be grated from frozen). Ginger paste/purée from jars may be used to replace freshly grated ginger. Use the same amount.

Herbs

Measurements of herbs refer to dried herbs, unless fresh herbs are specified. If you want to use fresh herbs, use about three time the quantity of the chopped fresh herb. While herbs add flavour to many recipes, they are seldom essential so, if necessary, leave out or replace with another herb.

Limes

Lime juice and freshly grated lime rind are much more strongly flavoured than fresh lemon juice and rind. Some stores now stock plastic bottles of unsweetened lime juice. Use in the same quantities as fresh juice (juice of one lime is approximately 2 teaspoons). Alternatively, lemons can usually be used in place of limes although the result will not be quite the same.

Oil and Butter

For flavour we use butter in preference to margarine, although for many recipes they may be interchanged. When it comes to oil we generally use olive and canola oils, which are higher in monounsaturated fats than most other vegetable oils. We fry foods in grape

seed oil as it is almost odour free. For health reasons we should use all fats and oils sparingly. Remember the food pyramid, do not use more butter or oil than you need in cooking, and keep rich fatty foods for occasional treats.

Pasta

Fresh pasta is now available from most supermarkets. It is very quick to cook and has a different texture from cooked dried pasta. Both are good in their own way — it is hard to beat dried pasta for convenience. Interestingly, the cooked yields for fresh and dried pasta are quite similar, 100g of uncooked fresh pasta gives 200g (1¼ cups) cooked, and 100g dried pasta gives 250g (1½ cups) cooked. Allow 75–100g uncooked pasta per main-sized serving.

Sesame Oil

Oriental (brown) sesame oil has a lovely roasted sesame seed flavour that it imparts to the recipe in which it is used. Colourless sesame oil has no flavour. Do not use it in the recipes in this book.

Star Anise

Star anise is a spice used in Asian cookery. A whole star anise 'flower' is made up of about eight 'petals'. Star anise is the most pungent ingredient of five-spice powder, so use a pinch of this to replace a 'petal' of star anise if need be.

Stock

Using stock instead of water gives extra flavour to some soups and sauces. You can make your own, buy 'tetrapak' stocks ready to use, or dilute concentrates or powders as per the instructions on packs. Instant stocks are salty, so take care not to make them too strong. If you save vegetable cooking liquids (up to two days in your refrigerator) you will have vegetable stock on hand. See Chicken Stock recipe (page 112). If you boil up chicken trimmings, bones, etc., after a meal, then freeze the stock in ice cubes, you will always have real stock on hand.

Tomato Paste

Tomato paste (22–24% tomato solids) is semi-solid and about twice as concentrated as tomato purée.

Tomato Purée

Tomato purée is a pourable liquid (10–12% tomato solids), about twice as concentrated as mashed, cooked tomatoes.

Vinegar

By adding a little vinegar, you often bring out the flavour of other ingredients. You can choose from several different vinegars. The mildest and the one most used in general cookery is wine vinegar. If you don't have wine vinegar on hand, use slightly less cider or other vinegar, or twice the volume of lemon juice. Balsamic vinegar is a very special wine-based, aged vinegar with a definite flavour of its own. It is used in small quantities. A few drops added to salads will bring them 'alive'. It is much more expensive than other vinegars, but keeps well. Replace with sherry vinegar (another specialist vinegar) or wine vinegar, if necessary.

Wine and Sherry

Small amounts of wine and sherry give extra flavour to cooking liquids. Replace these with diluted fruit juices, e.g. use 1 Tbsp lemon juice and 1 tsp sugar made up to ½ cup with water, or, ¼ cup orange juice plus ¼ cup water to replace ½ cup wine. Replace sherry with undiluted orange or apple juice. When wine mixtures are boiled, the alcohol is removed, and only the flavour remains.

GOOD NUTRITION

Good food is one of the great pleasures of life! As well, we need good food to grow, maintain our bodies, and give us the energy we need to get on with our lives.

We have so many foods available that it is sometimes hard to make the right selection. We need to choose foods which, together, will provide us with the protein, carbohydrates, fat, fibre, vitamins and minerals that we need.

Red meat is an important source of iron. Semi-vegetarians should be make sure that they eat other foods rich in easily absorbed iron, such as mussels, sardines and chicken livers, at regular intervals. Breakfast cereals fortified with iron, legumes, snacks of nuts, pumpkin and sunflower seeds and dried fruits contain iron too, as do bran, brewers yeast and wheatgerm, although this iron is not so easily absorbed. (Eat these foods with foods rich in Vitamin C for better absorbtion.)

Semi-vegetarians, like other groups, do not need to know exactly what is in everything they eat, but it *does* help to have an idea of the food groups from which a variety of foods should be chosen each day.

Vegetables and Fruit:
Select at least three servings of vegetables and two of fruit each day. (For extra iron, include dried fruits as snacks.)

Breads and Cereals:
Select at least six servings of foods made from cereals (grains) such as bread, breakfast cereals, pasta, rice and other grains each day. (Include some whole-grain products in your choices, and choose some breakfast cereals which are fortified with iron.)

Milk and Dairy Products:
Select at least two servings a day, preferably choosing reduced-fat milk, yoghurt and cheese.

Lean Poultry , Fish, Eggs, and Pulses:
Choose at least one serving from this group each day. Include iron-rich foods such as chicken livers, sardines and mussels regularly.

When you plan your daily food, remember that it is important not to eat too much fat, sugar and salt.

Keep a healthy weight with regular exercise as well as healthy eating.

INDEX

118

INDEX

INDEX